"Jan Johnson's *Abundant Simplicity* opens up an inviting spiritual path with clear explanations, rich references to a long Christian spiritual tradition, searching exercises in self-examination and piercing questions. Her vivid style and depth of perception help us to practice authentic simplicity and gain the abundant blessings of doing so. All under the power of God's grace."

Emilie Griffin, author of *Souls in Full Sail*

"Jan Johnson believes that an outwardly simple life yields great inner riches. Weaving together Scriptures, stories and practical suggestions, she paints an inviting picture of simplicity and encourages the reader to embrace this countercultural, yet fruitful, spiritual practice. Her winsome and engaging perspective is urgently needed today."

Lynne M. Baab, author of *Sabbath Keeping* and *Friending*

"What I find so engaging about *Abundant Simplicity* is the natural way Jan Johnson unfolds spiritual disciplines as partners in the abundant life of God. . . . The regular practice of asking our hearts, 'What is running me?' may not only reveal motives we're not proud of but also offer opportunities to lead a more peaceful, simple life."

Dr. Norvene Vest, author of *Gathered in the Word* and *Re-Visioning Theology*

"Jan Johnson writes in a clear style that seeks to make spirituality—following God's Spirit in daily life—more accessible to the reader. She challenges readers yet expresses sympathetic patience with the difficulty of practicing spiritual disciplines."

Gordon Houser, associate editor of *The Mennonite*

"For our hurried and harried existence, both within and without the church, Jan Johnson proposes fruitful pathways leading to a simpler and less cluttered lifestyle. *Abundant Simplicity* offers guidelines that commend to readers life-giving simplicity through protocols such as economy of speech (clipping our tongues), loosening our grip on possessions (frugality) and creating margins in life (leisure). The more I read, the more engrossed, convicted and encouraged I became to pursue the abundant life for the glory of God and the good of others."

Bruce Demarest, professor of Christian formation, Denver Seminary, and author of *Seasons of the Soul*

"In a world where *abundant* has come to mean prosperity and *simplicity* is often equated with scarcity, Jan Johnson proposes an alternative. She introduces us to a biblical lifestyle of fullness—full in ways that only God can fill. In our materialistic, over-scheduled, stress-filled world . . . we need to tame the monster called 'more.' *Abundant Simplicity* is a monster-tamer."

Paul Borthwick, author of *Simplify* and *Six Dangerous Questions to Transform Your View of the World*

"Once again writer Jan Johnson proves herself to be a wise, welcoming and eminently helpful guide as we follow Jesus day by day. *Abundant Simplicity* assists readers in taking a long, grace-imbued look into our deepest selves, discerning what within us is in keeping with our journey of faith, and then, by God's grace and spiritual discipline, discarding what is not. As Johnson demonstrates in theologically sound and practical ways, when we are winnowed toward holiness, what remains is, indeed, simple *and* abundant."

Susan S. Phillips, author of *Candlelight: Illuminating the Art of Spiritual Direction* and executive director, New College Berkeley

"Time and possessions, words and worries are the raw material that comprise daily life. They are also the places where students of Jesus often experience the 'simplicity gap'—the distance between their desire for simplicity and their experience of it. In *Abundant Simplicity* Jan Johnson wisely, gently and creatively demonstrates how that raw material of ordinary living can be transformed into extraordinary kingdom living through experiments and adventures in simplicity. This is a book of lived truth and uncommon yet *simple* wisdom."

Howard Baker, instructor of Christian formation, Denver Seminary, and author of *The One True Thing*

ABUNDANT SIMPLICITY

DISCOVERING THE UNHURRIED
RHYTHMS OF GRACE

JAN JOHNSON

IVP Books

An imprint of InterVarsity Press

Downers Grove, Illinois

InterVarsity Press
P.O. Box 1400, Downers Grove, IL 60515-1426
World Wide Web: www.ivpress.com
E-mail: email@ivpress.com

InterVarsity Press® is the book-publishing division of InterVarsity Christian Fellowship/USA®, a movement of students and faculty active on campus at hundreds of universities, colleges and schools of nursing in the United States of America, and a member movement of the International Fellowship of Evangelical Students. For information about local and regional activities, write Public Relations Dept., InterVarsity Christian Fellowship/USA, 6400 Schroeder Rd., P.O. Box 7895, Madison, WI 53707-7895, or visit the IVCF website at <www.intervarsity.org>.

Scripture quotations, unless otherwise noted, are from the New Revised Standard Version of the Bible, *copyright 1989 by the Division of Christian Education of the National Council of the Churches of Christ in the USA. Used by permission. All rights reserved.*

While all stories in this book are true, some names and identifying information in this book have been changed to protect the privacy of the individuals involved.

Cover design: Cindy Kiple
Interior design: Beth Hagenberg
Images: Mark Horn/Getty Images

ISBN 978-0-8308-3547-8

Printed in the United States of America ∞

Library of Congress Cataloging-in-Publication Data

Johnson, Jan, 1952-
  Abundant simplicity: discovering the unhurried rhythms of grace /
Jan Johnson.
      p. cm.
  Includes bibliographical references (p.   ).
  ISBN 978-0-8308-3547-8 (pbk.: alk. paper)
  1. Simplicity—Religious aspects—Christianity. 2. Christian life.
I. Title.
  BV4647.S48J65 2011
  241'.4—dc22

                                                      2010052969

P	18	17	16	15	14	13	12	11	10	9	8	7
Y	25	24	23	22	21	20	19	18	17			

CONTENTS

1

ABUNDANT LIFE WITH GOD

Do not store up for yourselves treasures
on earth, where moth and rust consume
and where thieves break in and steal;
but store up for yourselves treasures in
heaven, where neither moth nor rust
consumes and where thieves do not break in
and steal. For where your treasure is,
there your heart will be also.

Matthew 6:19-21

AS FOLLOWERS OF CHRIST, many of us would like to live a conversational life with God and be filled with a deeper sense of God's companionship. We'd also like to change—to be more kind and less crabby, more generous and less self-absorbed, more genuine and less forced.

If we want these things enough, we may start reading books and attending classes and retreats, practicing the disciplines usually taught there: solitude, silence, reflective prayer and meditative ways of reading Scripture. We often find these ways of relating to God to be nurturing and life-changing. We even talk about how we'll never read the Bible the same way again or how we're opening up to hearing God in our life. We want more!

But when we get back to normal life, our new techniques don't seem to work. The possibilities we saw before us fade away. Why can't we hold on to the genuine transformation we desire? Because we're trying to breathe in the oxygen of real life with God without breathing out the daily chaos that chokes out such interaction.

Experiments

One way to breathe out the frenzy of life is to weave disciplines of simplicity into our daily rhythms. Simplicity is the factor we most often overlook when we're seeking soul-nurturing companionship with God. It is the unstated component of a retreat that we can't easily practice at home or work. During a retreat, our speech is slower and simpler, perhaps even to the point where we become silent. Access to possessions such as clothing and electronics is limited, so we are less distracted. Time flows slowly and easily. Leisure abounds. Without realizing it, we are practicing disciplines of simplicity:

- simplicity of speech
- frugality
- spaciousness of time
- holy leisure
- simplicity of appearance and technology

Simplicity is not a discipline itself but a *way of being.* It is letting go of things others consider normal. It is an "inward reality of single-hearted focus upon God and [God's] kingdom, which results in an outward lifestyle of modesty, openness, and unpretentiousness and which disciplines our hunger for status, glamour, and luxury." We practice simplicity when we intentionally arrange our life around God—what he is doing in us and in this world—and let the rest drop off.

Such careful arrangement comes from following disciplines of simplicity, several of which we'll examine in this book. Within these disciplines, we can use specific practices to help us breathe out. You will find suggested ways to experiment with these simplicity practices at the end of each chapter. Along the way I'll introduce you to people who tried out such experiments and tell how these simple activities affected them. For example, Carol experimented with simplicity when several of her friends at work were giving things up for Lent. She

> By the end of the forty days, she'd forgotten about most of the things she wanted.

didn't ordinarily practice Lent, but the idea of simplifying drew her. To her husband's surprise, she gave up shopping. She still purchased groceries for her family once a week, but other than that she bought nothing for forty days.

Whenever Carol thought about something she wanted to purchase during that time, she said to God, "I'll let it wait. You are enough." By the end of the forty days, she'd forgotten about most of the things she wanted. Reflecting on her experiment, she notes, "I had more time for people because life was less hectic. Being in stores messes with your mind. It convinces you that you need things you don't need at all."

Carol's experiment with setting aside shopping also gave way to more daily conversation with God and created more space for loving others. She experienced more of the abundant life that humans were created to experience here and now— trusting God, abiding in Christ and living in terms of the Spirit (Mt 6:33; Lk 17:21). Living the moments of our days in this kingdom life brings about justice, joy and peace in the Holy Spirit (Rom 14:17).

Treasuring God

You may be reading this book because you want to learn how to slow down and be happy, live a rich life by spending less, or work smarter and not harder. While those things may occur as a natural result of simplicity, they are only byproducts. The point of simplicity is not efficiency, increased productivity or even living a healthier, more relaxed life. The point is making space for treasuring God's own self (Mt 6:19-21).

"The most important commandment of the Judeo-Christian tradition is to treasure God and his realm more than anything else," says philosopher and author Dallas Willard. "That is what it means to love God with all your heart, soul, mind, and strength. It means to *treasure* him, to hold him and his dear, and to protect and aid him in his purposes. Our only wisdom, safety, and fulfillment lies in so treasuring God." Disciplines of simplicity equip us to gather treasures in heaven, which Willard describes as investing our life in what God is doing, investing in our relationship to Jesus himself (and through him to God) and devoting ourselves to the good of other people— those within the range of our power to affect.

So the Christian focus of simplicity is to abide in Christ, or what we might call "hanging out" with God. As a result of this abiding, we organically manifest fruit such as love, joy and peace (Jn 15:4-5), which creates an obedience that is so empowered and remarkable that it surprises us (Jn 15:10-17). This is the true change we've been looking for.

Bloated Christians

Habits of simplicity help us connect with God in a way that is quite practical: They clear the mind and calendar to make room for better things, such as holy leisure and gut-level prayer. Without practices of simplicity, we wake up in the morning and begin filling our mind with a list of things to do. We can't pause because we feel driven to:

- be busy and be productive
- get going on all the things we've promised to do
- clean, fix and tidy up our possessions
- give our feedback about important situations
- participate in the frenzied quest for physical attractiveness

To limit the time and attention we spend on these things is not to miss out. In fact, it is a relief. A life of personal interaction and adventure with God gives rise to contentment. We realize we're satisfied with earning an adequate income and living in our current apartment or home. We see the beauty in ordinary things as a gift from God. We live life treasuring God and what he is doing today.

> Disciplines of engagement are like breathing in, and disciplines of abstinence are like breathing out. We need to exhale as well as inhale.

In the recent past, followers of Christ have mostly practiced disciplines of engagement, such as study, prayer, service, worship and fellowship. Disciplines of engagement help us take in the life of God. Disciplines of abstinence, however, such as fasting, solitude, silence, chastity, secrecy, frugality and simplicity of speech and time, help us let go of life-draining behaviors. We need to exhale what is unnecessary as well as inhale nourishment from God.

Practices of simplicity keep us from becoming bloated and swollen—unable to digest or use what we have taken in. Only as we say no to certain things do we create space to say yes to God and to live adventurous, abundant lives full of relationships and meaning.

This process of choosing the engaging, relational life we were built to live is described by Pedro Arrupe:

> Nothing is more practical than finding God, than falling in love in a quite absolute, final way. What you are in love with, what seizes your imagination, will affect everything.
>
> It will decide what will get you out of bed in the morning, what you will do with your evening, how you spend your weekends, what you read, whom you know, what breaks your heart, and what amazes you with joy and gratitude. Fall in love, stay in love, and it will decide everything.

Unchanged and Stuck

When people emphasize engagement disciplines to the neglect of abstinence practices, they may feel "filled up," but in reality they are likely to become agitated when things don't go their way or when others don't do what they want. They may know, practice and teach spiritual disciplines, but they still find themselves being impatient, egotistical or pushy.

This is because they have not blended engagement disciplines with abstinence disciplines, which prune away self-indulgence and willfulness—in other words, stubbornness (Jn 15:2). They train us to be sweet and content when we don't get what we want, whether it's a doughnut, a deserved recognition, a particular possession or others doing things our way.

If we don't practice abstinence disciplines regularly, we find ourselves stuck. We become reliant on our own devices (yelling, manipulation) to get people to do things, or we turn to inappropriate sources of satisfaction (our job, Internet porn). We're unable to experience transformation no matter how much we pray or meditate because there's all this stuff in us that needs undoing

We may not even be aware of the ingrained patterns of behavior we use to crush others and sabotage ourselves. We don't realize we're using words, possessions and busyness to feel important, to manage other people's opinions of us and, most of all, to get people to do what we want. An inner neediness of soul pushes us to indulge ourselves and get people to like us.

Think about how you felt the last few times you did something that led to twinges of regret: you said or spent too much, you tried too hard to impress someone, you put too much effort into trying to have fun, or you spent too many hours wandering the Internet or watching television because you were bored.

As life becomes more outwardly simple, it becomes more inwardly rich.

Simplicity disciplines empower us to temporarily give these things up. When we do, we see how deeply we have counted on them to (falsely) feel nurtured and acceptable. We also see how they suck up our time, drain our energy and create craziness in our inner life. Simplicity's undoing process creates space for God to work with our motives and thoughts. We begin to ask ourselves, *Can I let go of this grudge, this dessert, this role, this incredible phone and rely on God to meet my needs instead?* Then, once our neediness of soul becomes clear, we can turn to disciplines of engagement to find the specific kind of nourishment we truly need from God.

In this undoing process, we learn to rely on God minute by minute for practical things when we don't get what we think we

need or want. This greater dependence on God in turn reha-
bilitates patterns we don't want to think about. The change is
not punishing but freeing. We shed pretentious and forced ways
of speaking and spending time, energy and money. Choosing
what to buy and how to enjoy leisure becomes less complicated
because we make intentional and unadorned choices. We become clear-headed in our thinking.

As life becomes more outwardly simple, it becomes more inwardly rich. It also becomes more fun because we can focus on
one thing at a time without becoming stressed. With greater
satisfaction of heart, our sense of restlessness (*I'm bored . . . I
need to . . .*) disappears. We move toward contentment, finding
it easier to experience unexpected adventures with God as we
say yes to him in new ways.

More of Jesus, Less of Ego

Simplicity is an organic part of an interactive life with God, as
Sharon illustrates with this account:

> What happened was just the next step in our apprentice-
> ship to Jesus. Bob and I weren't trying to do anything he-
> roic or exemplary. We were simply trying to be wise in
> light of the kindness of God.
>
> It began because I had a longing for God that found
> intimacy in solitude, silence, fasting and contemplative
> reading. The books I was reading drew me to live a more
> generous life, by invitation and not by guilt. I wanted more
> of God and wanted to live in the kingdom now, not just
> talk about it. I began seeing Jesus as someone who cared
> about real people, not just about correct doctrine. As I
> talked with Jesus about what was on his heart, wealth
> seemed like it wouldn't make his top ten list.

Also, our worldly way of accumulation was not working. It turned out to be time-consuming. Achieving and maintaining the magazine home was an exhausting burden, even with help to keep it up. So my desire also arose out of failure as well as the gentle prodding of God.

The result was that Bob and I sold our house and scaled back. It has been so liberating. With the freed-up money, we were able to buy a smaller house for ourselves and also to hold the loan for a Congolese immigrant family we'd begun working with. With reduced economic pressures, we could give more. Once we started to live more simply, shopping became a waste of time because we didn't want more stuff to enter our house.

I also began eliminating activities. This freed up emotional space so that I was increasingly able to consider new ideas that came to my attention—ideas that seemed to be more on God's radar than my next tennis match. Tennis is fine, of course, but I was willing to give it up in order to have more of Jesus. Plus, I was a lousy tennis player!

As I experienced newfound freedom through simplifying my time and money, another thought wiggled into my mind: I could also be free of the compelling drive to demand my way (nicely, of course). Until this point, it seemed the only natural way to live. My practice of fasting confirmed it: I realized I was just fine without what I wanted (food). I started to test it out in other areas of life. Simplifying has been one of the greatest adventures I've ever experienced. Life has gotten more interesting, not less.

Sharon's journey began with a longing for God. She found it difficult to pass through the narrow door to life that is truly life (Mt 7:13-14; 1 Tim 6:19) when her arms were full of possessions, tasks and leisure activities. Sharon and Bob's decisions resulted not only in freedom from financial pressures but also in freedom to participate in the adventure of helping an immigrant family. Sharon also saw herself freed from that compelling drive to have her way. In letting go, she found she'd gained much more.

Examining the Heart

However, while simplicity disciplines bring freedom, they also make us feel uncomfortable, especially at first. They reveal the petty things we do to be noticed or to indulge ourselves. We may not have known we were hooked on luxuries, other people's attention or dressing to impress until we abstained from those things for a while. Then we find we've used them to prop ourselves up or push ourselves forward. We begin wondering, *Why does it devastate me to think about giving away this item? Why was it so important that I mention that accomplishment? Will I make a decent impression if my clothes don't make a statement?* Disciplines of simplicity help us realize that we don't yet trust God to help us feel acceptable when we're not managing what others think of us.

As an awareness of how we treasure things other than God comes to the surface, we ask ourselves (and God), *What have been the subtle payoffs of my busy schedule, gathering knowledge in a particular area or owning the latest technology?* We may discover that we're preoccupied with "impression management"—controlling what other people think about us. Disciplines of simplicity reveal the self-serving motives we thought only other people had: pride, greed and desires to control.

Self-awareness is central to transformation.

Without conversations in which we ask ourselves and God

these hard questions, our transformation will be short-changed. Self-awareness is central to transformation because it shows us what we truly treasure. Indeed, the devotional masters stressed the twin themes of knowing God and knowing ourselves in how the Spirit works within us.

If we are to journey toward Christlikeness, we need to know "what is"—what we are truly like today. When we're unaware of our faults, we're fooled into thinking external practices are enough. No. True abiding in Christ helps me see my internal absurdities and self-centeredness along with God's radiant beauty. The heart exams of simplicity disciplines help us recognize, surrender and begin to work through our shortcomings with God.

Perhaps it sounds too devastating to recognize our character defects this way. God gives us grace to be gentle with ourselves. The Holy Spirit makes us aware of our shortcomings not so that we'll feel guilty and force ourselves to shape up. (This doesn't work anyway; the distraction of guilt keeps us stuck and distances us from God.) Rather, the Spirit gives us insightful awareness so we have a place to start. God is not mad at us, but mad about us. God is a safe shelter in which we can face our underlying motives and determine our next steps.

> It's not about "getting it right" but about following Jesus because that's the wisest, most winsome thing we could ever do.

Without these heart exams, we live the life of a sleepwalker, which philosophy professor Tom Morris describes well: "getting up, dressing, eating, going to work, breaking for lunch, working some more, going home, eating again, watching TV, leafing through magazines, exchanging a few words with fellow family members in the house or with friends on the phone, changing for bed, and falling to sleep—just to repeat the same routine all over, and over and over, without ever thinking about what it all means or how life should be really lived."

I confess that some of my own experiments with simplicity have produced extreme disappointment when I discovered that I was obsessed with myself. I thought I was selfless, but in fact I was preoccupied with what others thought of me. I was tempted to go back to the sleepwalking life. But I also realized that no one—not God, not the angels and certainly not my husband—was surprised by the fact of my self-obsession. Only I was. And my disillusionment with my needy state only made my spirituality more about me when I wanted it to be more about God. My job was to ask God to show me the next small step and empower me to take it. Then I needed to continue being open to what God might say to me.

Our misguided motives do not need to surprise us. The big deal is never our own spiritual status; it's God. We need to get over ourselves and our inadequacies and let Jesus become the central figure on the computer screen of our minds. It's not about "getting it right" but about following Jesus because that's the wisest, most winsome thing we could ever do.

Mistakes That Distract

To keep focused on treasuring God, set aside these ways of thinking:

Trying too hard. All spiritual disciplines involve experimentation and adventure. They cause us to ask what it would look like to trust God enough to not promote ourselves by means of overcommitment and a hurried life. To *force ourselves* to try certain practices that others try or to try to *achieve* simplicity doesn't work. Such coercion defeats self-awareness because it requires us to numb ourselves in order to adhere to the rigors of the practice.

Perhaps more sadly, if we force ourselves to do these things and seem successful, we become self-righteous. We begin to think we're better than others because they haven't given up what we have. *See how frugal I am, especially compared to you!* Eventually, however, I come to resent you because I gave up certain things and you didn't, but now you get more attention than I do.

Simplicity disciplines may be especially challenging if we're hooked on looking good, feeling good, having people like us or not wanting people to misjudge us. In those cases, it's wise to ask God what practices would be most helpful and not force ourselves into simplicity martyrdom (throwing the cell phone into the fountain at the strip mall we've vowed never to frequent again). Keep in mind that God woos and draws us into unusual but appropriate practices of simplicity. From them (and the conversations with God they create) comes simplicity of life.

Thinking we have to add more activities to our life. Disciplines of simplicity cause us to arrange differently what we already do—whether it's speaking to others, spending money, scheduling our day or having fun—not to do more things. These different ways of living lift us out of bondage and help us relate to people in more genuine ways. We take on less, not more.

Thinking simplicity means cutting back. Practices of simplicity are about focusing inward. Every no to a shopping trip or a television show makes space for a yes to something else, even if it's just to be still and be glad that God is God. Any practice of simplicity, no matter how small, invites us to take a step on the path of treasuring God as we let go of other things.

In fact, simplicity leads to greater abundance in life. Because disciplines of simplicity create more space to experience fellowship with God, we no longer drag our impoverished selves to church every week to get "fixed" spiritually. For example, if we decide not to spend time on the Internet and take a walk instead, we have a chance to ask ourselves what we're most grateful for today (the prayer of *examen*). This process creates interaction with God and a sense of joy in being alive. Or if we choose not to go shopping but rather read a few verses of Scripture slowly and sit in them, we gain a sense of what God is inviting us into this day. With such a God-nurtured lifestyle, we don't need a maximum-style weekend experience to get us through the week. We begin trusting God's very own self in daily life so that when we fellowship with others at church, we have more to give (1 Cor 14:26). The abiding life overflows.

Feel free to tweak the suggested experiments offered at the end of each chapter if they seem too extreme. Start small. (Or if you're more experienced, tweak them so that they mess with your distractions and desires a little more.) Be alert that the Holy Spirit will help you come up with versions that fit you much better than anything I could suggest. It's OK to let go of things slowly: "Above all, trust in the slow work of God."

EXPERIMENTS WITH SIMPLICITY

- Think of one or two people you know who live simply. Note how simplicity helps them. (But also be honest with yourself—have you at times thought they were naïve?) Because simplicity, like goodness, is more caught than taught, speak with them about simplicity and see what they have to say.

- Meditate on Matthew 6:19-21. Why would Jesus speak of God as the treasure? Underline any ideas in the passage that lead you to believe that God being our treasure is a good idea. If you wish God to be your treasure, say that to God.

- Make plentiful use of this prayer of self-awareness: Search me, O God, and know my heart. Test me and know my anxious thoughts that drive me to distraction and excess. See if there is any offensive, ostentatious way in me and lead me in your glorious way everlasting (Ps 139:23-24, paraphrased to move toward simplicity and away from complexity). As you pray this prayer, rephrase it to suit what you discover as your self-awareness increases.

- Experiment with disciplines of abstinence by going without caffeine or sweets or chocolate for a few hours or days. Note how easy or difficult it is to be nice to people when you feel deprived.

QUESTIONS FOR DISCUSSION
AND REFLECTION

1. What stood out most to you in this chapter? Why?

2. Do you tend to let self-awareness help you or do you beat yourself up with it? If God were going to say something to you about self-awareness, what do you think it would be?

3. How do you respond to Sharon's story? What did you like or dislike about what she chose to do and what happened to her as a result?

4. Which of the traps about simplicity might you fall prey to, if any: forcing yourself to do certain practices, making simplicity one more thing to do, thinking this is just all beyond you?

5. What does this chapter lead you to want to pray?

2

COPING WITH PLENTY

I have learned to be content
with whatever I have.
I know what it is to have little,
and I know what it is to have plenty.
In any and all circumstances I have
learned the secret of being well-fed
and of going hungry, of having plenty
and of being in need.

Philippians 4:11-12

PEOPLE MARVEL THAT THE apostle Paul could be content while chained in a prison cell for years. This former Pharisee probably lived in filth and darkness, ridicule and loneliness. At best, his movements were restricted under house arrest by the Romans.

But it's just as bewildering that Paul was content in times of plenty. When he stayed with rich folks such as Philemon or Lydia, he didn't envy them or think, "Jesus was poor. Don't they know that?" When he moved on from their homes to less opulent situations he didn't think, "I sure do miss all that great food and the beautiful home." He was truly content with whatever he had.

Contrary to what we usually think, having plenty does not make us content. Instead, a taste of plenty makes us want a little more than what we've got. When offered an increase in salary, who among us would say, "No thanks. I'm content with what I have. I don't need a thing"?

We Want One Thing but Do Another

In a study on work, money and religion, sociologist Robert Wuthnow found that people feel worried about getting their personal needs met no matter how far up they are on the economic ladder. One person interviewed in his book said she earned a six-figure income but that it would take at least $50,000 more per year for her to live comfortably. Having plenty wasn't quite enough to live comfortably.

Those of us who follow Christ are often unaware of how these appetites injure our life with God. "We live in a materialistic culture, and we want money and possessions, and very few people have heard a powerful voice telling them to resist those impulses, or how to resist those impulses. . . . Organized religion . . . has not done a good job of challenging people to examine their lifestyles." Wuthnow found in interviews that religion is merely a therapeutic device designed to make people feel good about themselves. The church seems to have little to say about material consumption or self-indulgence.

Amid all this desire for more, however, many people also desire a simpler life, at least ostensibly. Take the magazine *Real Simple*, for example. While most new magazines fail, this one succeeded immediately. But a peek inside reveals pages and pages of advertisements and articles about new products—simplicity as a lifestyle to be purchased. The message is mixed:

desire simplicity, but buy more stuff to get it.

We resemble the Roman god of doors and gates, Janus, who had two faces turned in opposite directions. In Janus's case, this was an advantage so he could see the past and future at once. But our two faces represent divided minds as well; we desire a simpler life but we also think that the comfortable life we want can be acquired only by purchasing more things. Whichever face rules us in the moment seems to be unaware of the other. The I-need more face cannot see that its arms are already full of activities and purchases.

Cultural Awareness

In our journey together in this book, I'll describe common cultural messages about attractiveness, success and the so-called good life. I do this to help us become savvy about how these messages differ from the wisdom of our teacher, Jesus, and to subtly replace them with thoughts of treasuring God, investing our life in what God is doing and devoting ourselves to the good of other people.

The cultural messages described below—mostly about how success is defined as having more money, fame, power and status—are woven into our thoughts through exposure to the innumerable commercial messages that the average American experiences every day. Below are the assumptions behind those cultural messages. Their preeminence explains why we have to learn to be content. Consider reading these messages prayerfully and with openness, examining their inaccuracy but also observing if they have a sense of reality in your life.

More is better; bigger is better. As society pressures us to move forward and upward, we feel the need to continually upgrade: our computers, our education, our living space, the quality of our grass. Consider that a twenty ounce soda, now com-

monplace, used to be enormous. In 1976, when 7-Eleven tested
a thirty-two-ounce fountain drink at one of its locations, the
store sold out of its entire thousand-cup stock in one weekend.
Now a thirty-two ounce drink is small compared to the forty-
eight- or sixty-four-ounce options. In the same way, the standard sizes of restaurant plates, television screens, outdoor grills
and mattresses have increased without our noticing.

On a national level, we seek a continuously expanding economy, assuming that "the pursuit of self-interest will necessarily
lead to ultimate social good," as author Richard Foster says. But
we're discovering instead that the pressure of constant expan-
sion often leads to the exploitation of both God's world and
other people through false advertising and ill treatment of
workers, especially in developing countries by multinational
corporations.

Busyness is a sign of power and significance. If someone tells
us, "You're always so busy," they usually mean it as a compli-
ment. Busy people are important people, and we're supposed to
be flattered. In our society it's assumed that anyone who wants
to get ahead must attend power lunches and strategic social
events. These activities satisfy that drive that dictates to us—
though we're barely aware of it—*I need to be noticed, to get attention, to move ahead.*

All my desires must be fulfilled. When Thomas Jefferson
wrote about the right to life, liberty and the pursuit of happiness in the Declaration of Independence, he was thinking in
terms of not being locked up for being in debt or for being a
Baptist or a Quaker. But that phrase has morphed into the notion that we have a right to pursue whatever makes us happy.
For people in developed countries, freedom is no longer about
the absence of tyranny and oppression but about unrestricted
freedom of choice: You have no right to stop me from doing

whatever I want. As a result, people are mastered by their desires. The pursuit of happiness backfires, luring us to use people and love things.

We justify these actions through a deep-seated belief that our feelings must be satisfied. We even hear it said that to choose not to satisfy our desires is to warp our sense of self: *I wouldn't be me*. This message stood out to me many years ago during a television show in which a woman (whose character I otherwise admired) advised her unmarried, unattached daughter something like this: "You're just grouchy because you haven't had sex lately."

> The pursuit of happiness backfires, luring us to use people and love things.

Think about that for a moment: According to this mindset, kindness isn't possible without recent sexual experience. The mother believed that the daughter was harming herself by not satisfying her feelings. In this way of thinking, to resist feelings or to replace them with other feelings is out of the question. Feelings of lust and anger, in particular, are not only accepted but also applauded in movies, books and talk radio.

I Can't Resist

The use of humor and sentimentality in advertising makes this deadly message of self-indulgence seem less harmful than it is—even funny or cute. Self-indulgence grows when we give in to excess, often by spending money or eating certain foods. We repeatedly give in until that activity becomes a settled behavior and we're unable to resist gratifying even the smallest whim. Giving in to small, seemingly benign, culturally acceptable temptations leads to enslavement. People of faith are not exempt; those in whom the Word of God has been sown may find that the "care of this world . . . and deceitfulness of riches" choke out the life of God in them (Mt 13:22 KJV).

For example, I've always wondered how King David could commit adultery with Bathsheba and murder her husband when he lived such a faithful life overall; he was a man after God's own heart (1 Sam 13:14). But while reading his whole story again recently, I saw that this evil didn't come out of nowhere. For David's entire adult life he practiced polygamy over and over in violation of God's law, marrying six wives and keeping numerous concubines (2 Sam 5:13; 1 Chron 3:1). Every time he took a wife or concubine he gave into the enslavement of that inner voice: *I must have her!* Committing adultery (and having to cover it up) was the next logical step.

Self-indulgence is self-destructive. It destroys integrity one good intention at a time and eats away at the capacity to think about loving God and others. Self-indulgence invites us to be not only in the world, as Jesus was, but also of the world, with character and habits that look just like everybody else's (Jn 1:10; 9:5; 17:11; 1 Jn 2:15-16).

Disciplines of simplicity are powerful because they move us away from self-indulgence just for today: don't buy this one thing; don't sign up for one more activity; don't mention this last accomplishment to anyone. Even when we practice these restraints only temporarily, they still train us not to grab what we want now. In the midst of our discomfort during these little experiments, something beautiful happens within us: the enormous river barge of our life that's flowing toward self-indulgence is turned around and begins to move upstream toward self-giving Christlikeness.

Simplicity practices chip away at self-indulgence by interrupting our reflexive habit of doing whatever makes us happy. They make us aware of our excesses: driving five miles out of my way to have my favorite hamburger instead of eating whatever is handy; checking phone messages now because I can't pay attention one more second to this long-winded person talking to me. To set limits by eating simply or checking phone messages only twice a day teaches us to die to self when we automatically reject the urge to insist on getting what we want when we want it.

Such little decisions toward selflessness are so nurturing that pioneering psychologist and philosopher William James advised us to deny ourselves a little something each day. Then when our will is truly thwarted, we don't become crabby or manipulative. We respond in faithful, loving ways rather than seeking revenge or simmering with quiet resentment.

Slowly but Surely

As we follow God's grace-filled invitations into disciplines of simplicity, we learn to be content and to resist the impulse for more. To our surprise, our personality becomes progressively more organized around God and the way God moves in the world.

That progression proved to be true in Cathleen's life. She says,

> When I was young, I street-raced for years. Expensive and powerful cars were important to my identity. But I surrendered that to the Lord and was glad to let my husband pick out whatever car worked best for our family. Recently when I needed a car and he suggested we buy our son's Lexus (so it would still be available to him for occasional business use), I agreed because I saw it was the best option for our entire family.
>
> At first, driving a Lexus was no big deal. I was over the expensive car addiction. I even felt guilty when I drove it to my spiritual director's house. Would she think I'd sold

out and was still hooked on the world? But I also began enjoying the sense of self-importance. Other drivers
treated me respectfully. To be honest, I thought I was finally worthy. Then I became self-conscious because it was
an older model; did people think I couldn't afford a newer
model? When I found two of the fancy *L*'s missing from
the wheel covers, they had to be replaced immediately.

As I worked through this, the hardest part was that I
thought I'd laid to rest these issues of identity and self-
worth. Back when I'd surrendered having a powerful car,
I couldn't have it. Now that having a luxury car was appropriate and helpful, I couldn't enjoy it because of my
inner turmoil. It took a year to wrestle through these issues, and now it's just a car again, serving only my trans-
portation needs. I'm grateful for freedom from the driven-
ness, and freedom to do the simple thing.

Notice how Cathleen's conversations with God made this experience a place of growth. First, God invited her into a simplicity that was away from fast cars (coping with less, or what
seemed like less). Then years later God invited her to drive a
Lexus for the convenience of her family (coping with plenty).
When being a Lexus driver became her master, she saw she had
to revisit with God her issues of identity and self-worth.

Observe how the hardest part for Cathleen was that she'd
thought she was finished finding her identity and self-worth in
cars. And she had actually done quite well in her earlier years.
But now she and God were conversing at a deeper level of ma-
turity, and she had the capacity to hear more complex things.
(God is gentle that way, telling us only what we can stand to
hear in that moment of our growth.) She wrestled with this,
which illustrates the importance of the heart examination that

goes on while experimenting with disciplines of simplicity.

> God tends to be gentle, telling us only what we can stand to hear in that moment of our growth.

Because these conversations took place in the midst of knowing that God treasured her as much as she treasured God, Cathleen experienced the freedom to work through her identity and self-worth and find them once again in God, but this time in a much deeper way. In other words, she didn't fail. She moved forward and God was glad to meet her there.

Two Masters

Jesus, a master of logic, tells us it's impossible to live like the two-faced god of doors and gates, Janus. He calls it serving two masters (Mt 6:24). And he says it's not just that we shouldn't do it; we cannot. We are not able to do it. Our actions, especially those of which we're unaware (but everyone in our household has known about for years), reveal which master we truly serve. That master gets our time, energy and paycheck. It might be high productivity, admiration from others, technological savvy, having fun, building a strong body, or being perceived as a deep thinker.

The bad news is that marketing folks have identified these masters we don't know we're serving. "Marketing theory says that people are driven by fear, by the promise of exclusivity, by guilt and by greed, and by the need for approval. Advertising . . . promises to resolve our discomfort with a product." This happens fifty to a hundred times before nine a.m. every day.

Advertising also plays into our fears that we won't have enough, that we'll miss out, that we'll be shown to be inadequate, that we'll be misjudged, rejected and left out, that we'll face others' disapproval, anger or disappointment. These fears, which focus on not being loved or valued, are evidence of an internal neediness that holds us back and that God invites us into conversation about.

If you listen to the stress inside you as you try the experiments suggested in this book, you may discover a neediness in your own soul you didn't know existed. This neediness may have resulted from past wounds that have left you feeling more fearful or angry than you realize. These wounds need to be explored and addressed, a process that often occurs in stages, as Cathleen's story illustrates. You may have found healing and made progress with the help of a therapist, counselor or support group, but these fears may recur in other forms. In the meantime it's important to dream and ponder, *What would my life be like if I weren't afraid? What if I chose to trust God a little more today?*

The good news is that as Jesus progressively invades our "interior castle" (as Teresa of Avila calls the soul), he ties up the "strong man" who lives there. Jesus replaces that strong man with God's presence, room by room (Mk 3:27). This process happens partly through the practice of disciplines of simplicity. As we face the strong man of our past fears, we make small, incremental decisions about trusting God a little more. And more healing occurs.

Transformative growth works in a spiral, as it did with Cathleen. She had made great progress letting God's love for her be the basis of her identity and self-worth, but her neediness showed up again when she started driving the Lexus. As we're ready, God allows basic issues to resurface, but each time he lets us see ourselves more clearly so that better and deeper pruning work can be done. If we're wise, we'll make notes about what we're learning (in a jour-

Transformative growth works in a spiral.

nal, with a friend or therapist, or embedded in our memory) so we can look back and remember what we've learned when we work through it with God the next time.

Heart Exam: What Do You Want?

Facing our underlying fears prepares us to sit down and examine the central questions of life, the first of which are the core issues at the heart of the spiritual exercises of Ignatius of Loyola:

- What do I want?

- What do I really want?

- What am I longing for?

Jesus asked these same questions in many forms: "What do you want me to do for you?" (Mt 20:32), "What are you looking for?" (Jn 1:38) and "Do you want to be made well?" (Jn 5:6). He seemed to know that it was good for people to speak forth these core longings.

When asked to voice what we want, we usually offer admirable goals about living for God or serving our family or helping others. Those are our stated, realized goals. Disciplines of simplicity, however, reveal unstated, yet-to-be-realized goals: I want to be liked; I want to be noticed. In trying to discern these darker hidden goals, we might ask ourselves: By what standard do I measure others? What do I most dread losing? How do I spend most of my time, energy and money?

This last question touches on the concept of "revealed preference." As economics professor Bruce Wydick explains, "I can tell what you really value by how you use your resources. . . . Thus, we may say we have a magnanimous Christian love for everyone in the world, but if 99 percent of our time and energy is spent fighting to improve our own economic circumstances, who (or what) do we truly value? Our actions reveal our priorities."

So I may want to treasure God and think that I do (my stated goal), but my underlying goals may be revealed by how my

- online banking record shows that I spend nearly all my discretionary funds on products to help me look younger

- calendar shows that I spend a lot of time attending events that either win others' approval or increase others' esteem for me

- low energy level tells me that I put up with a job saturated by self-serving values because it pays good money

These insights reveal to us our underlying fears of not being loved and valued. So we have a few more conversations with God: What truths does God want to communicate to me today? How might the Spirit help me absorb these truths?

When our stated and unstated goals don't match (which is normal, so please don't beat yourself up if this is true of you), we need to consider: If I don't like what my actions tell me about what I want, what do I *want* to want?

If we want to want God, our next step is to come to terms with our underlying fears. We start where we are. We invite God to work with us on these fears so we can begin drinking God's living water, God's own Spirit, which, as Dallas Willard explains, "will keep [us] from ever again being thirsty—being driven and ruled by unsatisfied desires. . . . Indeed, it will even become 'rivers of living water' flowing from the center of the believer's life to a thirsty world (Jn 7:38)."

Skipping the heart exam puts us in grave danger of making simplicity practices about external behavior only. The Pharisees partially ruined fasting and Sabbath-keeping by making them external practices without looking within. They did not practice these disciplines with an openness to hearing God speak or to discern God's invitations for today.

Getting There

Realizing the difference between our unstated goals and what we want to want takes time, thought, humility, objectivity and openness to the Spirit's help in listening to oneself. Please read those elements again, slowly:

- time

- thought

- humility

- objectivity

- openness to the Spirit's help

God in enormous grace empowers us in this effort.

The *simple* way to experience these moments of clarity regarding our true motivations is to practice disciplines of simplicity. However, we can also experience them in a painful way when someone we love (or don't love) confronts us with the truth or when we fail to achieve our unstated goals. I believe that practicing disciplines of simplicity saves ourselves and others the pain of some of those confrontations and failures because these moments of realization occur daily as we deny ourselves in small ways as William James suggested. We need to process through these moments in a journal or by talking with a friend, counselor or spiritual director, and we also need to pray about them with intentionality.

Please don't think this process is bleak. In fact, it's exciting because Jesus is our companion on the journey. Our admiration for Jesus causes us to keep choosing to be his disciple as we (internally) desire more than anything to be like him and (externally) arrange our life to bring this about. We develop a personal strategy that usually includes spiritual disciplines targeted at places of growth the Spirit reveals.

Then we're ready to fill our minds with the real treasure of Christ and to become his hands and feet to our family, our friends and the needy. We start agreeing with Gregory of Nyssa, who said, "Disregarding all those things for which we hope and which have been reserved by promise, we regard falling from God's friendship as the only thing dreadful and we consider becoming God's friend the only thing worthy of honor and desire."

EXPERIMENTS WITH SIMPLICITY

- Explore the website www.adbusters.org and notice how its images communicate our enslavement to spending. (If nothing else, check out its "Buy Nothing Day" campaign.) What feelings do those images create in you?

- Read Matthew 6:24 slowly every day for a week, and ask God to show you the masters your actions reveal. What do you learn about what you want but have never stated explicitly? If you're really brave, ask a friend or someone you live with to suggest what your masters are. Try to smile at what this person says.

- Read Philippians 4:11-13. Then sit back and picture the apostle Paul chained in a cell yet just as content as the day he ate a huge meal at Philemon's house. What might he have thought about then? Consider Paul's contentment with plenty and with scarcity.

- Journal about this question: What do you want? First, write down what you think you want (your stated goals). Then ask God to help you search yourself as you look at your spending records and calendar. Consider your thought energy: What do you think about a lot?

- Consider the same question, but instead talk it through with a very trusted friend. Or go somewhere private and speak about it as if you were talking to a friend.

QUESTIONS FOR DISCUSSION AND REFLECTION

1. What stood out most to you in this chapter? Why?

2. How would you like to see your life progressively more organized around God and his eternal life?

3. How appropriate or inappropriate is your desire to be loved and valued?

4. What does this chapter lead you to want to pray?

5. Which of the above experiments do you see yourself trying out this week?

3

WHAT DO YOU REALLY WANT?

*The light of the body is the eye: if therefore
thine eye be single, thy whole body
shall be full of light. But if thine eye be evil,
thy whole body shall be full of darkness.
If therefore the light that is in thee
be darkness, how great is that darkness!*

Matthew 6:22-23 KJV

EVEN WHEN WE TRULY desire to live day to day in the companionship of God, we get distracted. We make a good start after reading a book or taking a class, but then a friend says, "Sure, trim your schedule, but our weekly lunch date is still on, right?" Or we plan to spend some time on the back porch enjoying the stillness or talking with our spouse, but a television show comes on about the latest celebrity mishaps and . . . well, we need to know what everyone's talking about, right? This distracted life is now considered not only normal but optimal. We're supposed to multitask; if we don't, we'll get behind.

Simplicity, however, can flow only when we embrace the opposite of distraction: intentionality. To be intentional means to have some kind of plan for moving forward. After we've thought about what we want, what we really want, even what we long for, we ask God to show us how we can begin to rearrange our lives to make more space for him. Such planning, even if we're planning only the next step, works against enslavement. That is why each chapter in this book ends with experiments for you to consider. Please intentionally choose—in a prayerful, reflective way—one or more and ask God to lead you into them with power and grace.

Intentionality doesn't come automatically for people who love God. We need to be invited into it and want it. Consider the Israelites. You'd think that after they were freed from bondage in Egypt, escorted through dangers in the desert and led to make the Promised Land their own, their choice of Yahweh would have been a foregone conclusion. But Joshua, their discerning leader, knew it was not. "Choose this day whom you will serve," he challenged them (Josh 24:15). In effect, he was saying, now that the dust has settled, what do you really want? This day and every day: What are you longing for?

When Israel accepted the challenge, Joshua told them to be intentional by putting away foreign gods (Josh 24:23). This would have been a difficult request for these Egyptianized wanderer-warriors who probably thought securing a little more gratuitous luck in their new land was not a bad idea. As time passed, God tested their intentionality, deciding not to drive out any of the nations Joshua left in Israel when he died, to see if they "would take care to walk in the way of the LORD as their ancestors did" (Judg 2:22). They did not.

The Single Focus
Jesus created several images to help us with the idea of intentionality. One of these is an undistracted gaze focused singly

on God. "If therefore thine eye be single, thy whole body shall be full of light" (Mt 6:22 KJV). This challenge, "If thine eye be single," is the foundation on which disciplines of simplicity rest. We allow purity of heart to grow by willing one thing only—an ever-expanding life with God. Fall in love with God and let that "decide everything," as Pedro Arrupe said. The single-minded

> The single-minded person does the next small thing that is needed.

person does the next small thing that is needed in order to focus on God instead of giving in to the automatic responses of the past. To treasure God is to have a single-focused life (Mt 6:19-23).

The mistake we make with intentionality is to view it as rigid resolve in which we clench our fists or hunch our shoulders, repeating every ten minutes, "I've got to do this. I will do this." Jesus' picture is different. His intentionality is a longing that comes from deep within. It shows itself as an eye that doesn't stray from the One it wants, or is learning to want.

This longing comes from gentle yet gut-level conversations in which God asks us, "What do you really want?" and then listens to us. This longing, solidified into intentionality, is actually a beautiful response to God's longing for us. Before the foundation of the world, God thought of each of us and thought each of us was a good idea (Eph 1:4-6). God longed for us even then.

Intentionality is turning our gaze to God and saying, "Yes. I want to be wanted. Show me what's next." We say yes to the One who has already done all the heavy lifting in the relationship: creating us, wooing us, sacrificing for us and building kingdom space for us. God's desire for us ignites the spark of our desire for God. We get to choose to respond to God's desire.

So if you find yourself in a spirit of rigidity—gotta, gotta,

gotta—at any time while reading this book, please come back to this space of sensing God's longing. Intentionality is about responding to the longing of God inviting you into a different kind of life.

Another picture Jesus offered, one we've already examined, is that of a poor soul who is worn out trying to serve two masters at the same time (Mt 6:24). We compared this to the Roman god of gates, Janus, who gazes in two opposite directions. We underestimate the pain and confusion we cause ourselves when we try to do the impossible task of gazing in opposite directions, especially when one direction is toward the God who longs for us and invites us to respond. It's exhausting to

- focus one eye on colaboring with God and another on whether I'm getting the credit I deserve

- keep one eye focused on helping those God nudges me toward and the other on whether they might do something advantageous for me

- tell the truth as God invites me to do but also worry that I will be misjudged for it

- know the work I truly want to do but apply for another job because it makes much more money

Laying Aside Distractions

Lack of intentionality—scattering our time and energy among things that don't fit with what we really want—will frustrate us because we sense we're not responding to God's longing. It will also work in us a mediocre character so that we have little effect on others and the wider world. It seems like no big deal to cram our schedule with as many events as we're invited to, to talk about ourselves a little too much or to spend a little too much money to brighten up our day. But these small things blur our focus and weigh us down.

Disciplines of simplicity invite us to "lay aside every weight" that hinders us (Heb 12:1). Sometimes those weights aren't bad things. This was evident in Paul's life. Before he burst forth with that intentional, determined declaration, "I want to know Christ and the power of his resurrection" (Phil 3:10; picture him saying this with his arms spread wide or raised high in the air), he first explained that he had laid aside the helpful weights of his rich heritage—the fact that he was circumcised on the eighth day, a Hebrew of Hebrews and so on (Phil 3:4-6). Formerly, these blessings were a "profit" but he came to consider them a "loss." Once he had cast them aside, he was ready for the treasure of knowing Christ.

One "good" weight that keeps us from simplicity is the desire to be up to date. This longing forces us to be double-minded as we try to focus on two things at once: the task in front of us today and the research, shopping and time required to break in the latest technology or technique. Another "good" weight is devotion to change. In his well-known essay "Purity of Heart Is to Will One Thing," nineteenth-century philosopher and theologian Søren Kierkegaard said that the craving for variety "is to will a multitude of things" and double-minded people need to purify their hearts from this. This constant desire for change, he said, is only for the purpose of satisfying one's pleasures.

It's true that variety and change can be good, but constantly chasing them can enslave us and numb our longing for God. We often favor change and variety without asking important questions, such as whether this new way will help us know God better or empower us to treat people better. Let's say I want to spend more time serving an ailing friend, but I'm short on time. I figure out I can save time in meal preparation by fixing a large dinner one night and then eating the rest of it through-

out the week. Saving food-prep time allows me to care for my
friend. But if variety in eating is a priority for me, it might seem
like too big a sacrifice.

If we choose to journey with God carrying unnecessary
weights, God will let us do it. God does not force us to lay unnecessary burdens down. But transformation into Christlikeness is much more difficult when we're encumbered by multi-
plicity of words, cluttered schedules, decathlon vacations or the
cell phone surgically attached to our ear. Cross-country run-
ners can cross a finish line wearing a
twenty-pound backpack or trailing
tangled shoelaces, but the race is
much more difficult. Expect God to
continually woo you to cast aside that backpack full of distractions and securely tie those shoes so that nothing pulls you
away from living your life with God.

> Expect God to
> continually woo you to
> cast aside distractions.

Love for God Decides Everything

John Woolman, an eighteenth-century Quaker, understood intentionality. Although he began as a vain young man who tried
to "promote mirth" (perhaps he joked at others' expense or be-
haved as the class clown), the power of Christ eclipsed his self-
ish desires. He began spending time in solitude, and when he
eventually entered into trade as a tailor and shopkeeper, he refused to sell goods that weren't useful. He didn't want to promote in others the vanity he had worked to overcome. In spite
of limiting his merchandise selection, he had an inclination for
business and became more and more successful. No doubt people expected him to expand his business, but instead he cut
back because he wanted to focus elsewhere.

Woolman seems to have responded to a longing for God and
then asked himself, *What do I want?* He realized that he wanted

to spend time traveling to other meetings of Friends, as Quakers were called, hundreds of miles away. So he shut down the merchandising side of business and worked mainly as a tailor. He decided to live in a "plain way" because he noticed that "with an increase of wealth the desire of wealth increased."

This New Jersey frontiersman also worked as a scrivener, which meant he wrote up wills and legal documents. He'd begun to feel uneasy about slavery, so he refused to finish a will or accept any payment if the will's provisions included turning over unfreed slaves to another person. He didn't worry about loss of money but explained his position briefly, and many clients agreed to free their slaves as a result.

As Woolman's preaching missions made him more acquainted with slaves' conditions, which he wept over, he began urging Friends to give up their slaves. He became a humble but dynamic force in this effort. One evening after preaching against slavery at a Quaker meeting, he was taken to the home of Thomas Woodward for dinner. Once there, he asked about the status of the servants and was told they were slaves. He quietly got up and left the home without a word. Woodward was so affected by this that he freed all his slaves the next morning.

Although Woolman lived in the mid-seventeen hundreds before the American Revolution (much less the Civil War), he already sensed that slavery was wrong and did what he could to stop it. He was not always well received by his fellow Friends, but he chose not to be disturbed by this. He did not live to see the end of slavery, but by 1787 no American Quaker owned a slave. I can't help but wonder if his clarity about slavery's evil so far ahead of his time was related to the simplicity of his life. Without the distractions of an abundance of possessions or the heavy burden of a successful business, he saw all people as created in God's image.

This gentle family man had a single-focused eye toward investing his life in God's own self and in what God was doing. He devoted himself to the good of those around him and also to those within the range of his power to affect. His actions were marked with stark self-awareness, a lack of self-indulgence and a single-focused devotion. As a result, he lived an adventurous life full of interaction with God.

Interrupting Automatic Pilot

The opposite of living intentionally as a response to God's longing is living on autopilot, which means doing whatever occurs to us without pausing to consider what we really want. It seems easier to do what we've always done or what everyone else does. Even if you learn to live intentionally, expect that in a time of crisis you'll switch to old automatic pilot choices. Plan ahead for this to happen and be vigilant.

Disciplines of abstinence interrupt automatic actions—not dipping my hand into the trail mix bag because I'm fasting from snacks or not turning on the music or television or computer when I come home because I'm fasting from media. This is how "by the Spirit [we] put to death the [automatic] deeds of the body" (Rom 8:13). If we're not sure whether a tendency is automatic, we can try disrupting it: asking a family member to hide the trail mix bag or putting tape over every "on" button in our living space.

In the pause of the interrupted moment, we have an important inward conversation with God: How does it feel not to get what we want? Empty? Frustrating? Lonely? What do those feelings tell us about what runs our life? Wise Jeremy Taylor, a seventeenth-century Anglican clergyman, advised, "In every action reflect upon the end; and in your undertaking it, consider why you do it, and what you propound to yourself for a reward, and to your action as its end." To "reflect upon the end" is to have an inward conversation with God about what we really want.

Intentionality means replacing autopilot by living "deliberately," as Henry David Thoreau called it. He found simplifying his life so difficult that he built himself a small cabin in the woods surrounding Walden Pond and started over with nothing. He carefully added only what he truly needed. "I wished to live deliberately . . . and see if I could not learn what it had to teach, and not, when I came to die, discover that I had not lived . . . to live deep and suck out all the marrow of life." To live deliberately means to move slowly, to look people in the eyes when they speak to us and to follow up on the ideas that the Spirit has possibly nudged us with. We find more satisfaction in this than in getting things done (being productive), acquiring more things or obtaining others' approval.

Most people do not begin practicing simplicity in such an extreme way as Thoreau, but it's good to consider the wisdom of his mindset: everything is open to question; we start with nothing on our schedule, to-do list, vacation plan or shopping list, and we add things deliberately and slowly. As we favor deliberate life choices over blind consumption and compulsion, we stop doing just whatever other people—even church people—do. We find rest in keeping our focus on loving God and joining God in loving others.

> As we favor deliberate life choices over blind consumption and compulsion, we stop doing just whatever other people—even church people—do.

Courage to Make Choices

Living with intentionality requires the courage to go against the grain of culture. "If you and I are to be made by God into people for God's purposes, it will depend largely on the courage with which we respond to God," wrote Evelyn Underhill. "It won't be worked by God's action alone. . . . It works through our brave and willing cooperation, our *active* acceptance and use of all the material we are offered, even everything that damages our vanity and opposes our self-will." Courage helps us choose how we will bravely and willingly cooperate, and spiritual practices are the material we are offered. Courage also invites us to let our pride and self-will be opposed and even to laugh at our silly, self-preoccupied tendencies.

Larae speaks about the intentionality required in her experiments with simplicity. She began by

> thinking and praying about priorities (*e.g.*, God, ministry, family, health, the environment, frugality) and simplifying every area of life toward them. There are a lot of ways I can spend my time, but do they help me meet my priorities? I may need to leave behind good things to give more effort to better things. One example is not teaching Sunday school because God is leading me to put more energy and focus into leading worship. Simplicity is all about intentionality.

Contrary to the tagline of the magazine *Real Simple*, which reads "Life made easier," Larae says,

> Simple does not always mean easier, but I think it means better. Going to Burger King for dinner is easier, but not necessarily better or more healthy than a home-cooked meal where the family can sit together and talk.
>
> Simplicity in finances is not being frugal for its own sake but in order to free up money to put into ministry or wherever God leads. Simplicity means being intentional

with fewer friendships instead of trying to get to know everyone. It means not always having the radio on in the car so God has a chance to speak to me. It means planning meals so I'm not wasting time making extra trips to the store. It means limiting the number of toys that require batteries, partially for the environment but also to have toys that challenge my child's imagination and creativity. Simplicity strips away the things that distract us (sometimes good things), helps us reevaluate where our heart is and provides room for God to speak.

Larae has done the soul-searching work of self-awareness and reaped the contentment of breathing out deeply so she can breathe in the life to which God is inviting her.

Benefits of Intentionality

Courageous, intentional decisions toward simplicity make space for God in ways that surprise us and change the tone of our life. Here are some of those ways.

Tranquility. Intentionally focusing on just a few things helps us not become overwhelmed by life. "When people control or entirely set aside materialistic desires, when they let go of raging ambition, and when they challenge media-generated paranoia, they no longer feel torn in a hundred directions," writes Paula Huston in *The Holy Way.* "Interior chaos subsides; the psychic battlefield goes calm and silent. People can experience themselves as whole and at peace instead of fragmented." Her phrase "psychic battlefield" aptly describes the turmoil with which many people begin their days as they wonder how they'll possibly get everything done.

Integration. Intentionally focusing on God's invitations to us helps the pieces of our life fit together better. For example, if we donate to the same organizations where we volunteer, we're more confident that our time and money are making a difference in the places God is calling us to invest.

Relating better to people. Disciplines of simplicity improve our relationships because we pay better attention to people. In a Los Angeles college-prep charter school, one homeroom teacher instituted a media fast for students for seven days: no iPods, iPhones, Blackberrys, computers (hence no MySpace or Facebook) or cell phones (which meant no text messaging). In this teen culture of "I tweet, therefore I am," some of the students "discovered they have younger brothers and sisters," says a reporter who covered the event. One student connected with her autistic brother. Another read a book for the first time that year. Still another reported that since she wasn't wearing headphones all the time, she now heard strange chirping sounds outside her window. These students learned a great deal about loving people instead of media. No one taught them; they learned it by living it—which is how spiritual practices work.

It's interesting to note that although this media fast was probably not spiritually motivated, disciplines of simplicity help people become less self-absorbed and more attentive to others and the world around them. Lack of self-indulgence moves us away from self-preoccupation. These students not only began noticing people and nature, but no doubt their bodies received enormous benefits from relaxation and their concentration improved with this rest.

Relating better to nature. The way the student above noticed strange chirping sounds outside her window shows how simplicity helps our connection with nature to grow. Simplicity of leisure (we'll address it in chapter eight) ushers in the lost art of porch- or balcony-sitting, which in turn allows us to enjoy sunsets and talk with our neighbors who pass by.

Authenticity. Living with tranquility, integration and connectedness to others and nature helps us be content with our unadorned self—the authentic self that does not need to impress anyone. This authenticity is possible because simplicity erodes our bent toward duplicity. "Simplicity is freedom. Duplicity is bondage," writes Richard Foster. "Simplicity brings joy and balance. Duplicity brings anxiety and fear." Duplicity is a form of deceit in which we defraud others by trying to be someone we're not. It's using words, possessions and time for "impression management" to convince others we're smarter or more talented than we really are. It may even involve exploiting people so we can get what we want. Duplicity leads to bondage as we become enslaved to our schedules and others' expectations. Eventually our inability to measure up to the lie we've created produces anxiety and fear.

Trying to be all things to all people means we have to squeeze in another appointment or errand. This may seem like no big deal except that we become so rushed and distracted that our real

> People find us easier to be around when we live in simplicity.

self of love and truth doesn't have space to show up. Disciplines of simplicity allow us to love others because we're no longer trying to manipulate them into doing what we want. We value people more and possessions less. We can look someone in the face and love that person genuinely because we're not hung up on whether our jeans make us look fat.

People also find us easier to be around when we live in simplicity. We are refreshingly absent of pretense or affectation. The real me has the chance to connect with the real you. But interacting with duplicitous people is exhausting. We have to guess what they really mean because they're not straightforward. Such game-playing clutters the mind.

We also find it easier to be around ourselves. We can behave as the same person all the time: the same person speaking on the platform as speaking one on one off the platform; the same person during a family dispute as the one who's cheerful with neighbors; the same person at a church meeting as at a business meeting. There's enough space for all of life to be lived with God.

Now as we move to the chapters on disciplines of simplicity—which is what some of you have been waiting for—consider how God treasures us and invites us into a life of interaction and conversation. Is this what we want? What we really want? If so, are we willing and even excited about making progress in our single focus on the God whose eyes are singly focused on us (Ps 17:8)? If so, read on.

EXPERIMENTS WITH SIMPLICITY

- Think of someone you know who lives with simplicity of intention and purity of affection, someone who is refreshingly absent of pretense or affectation. What is that person's life like? What is it like to be around that person? (If you can't think of a real person, then identify a character in movie or a book.)

- Read Matthew 6:19-23 slowly. Then meditate on verses 22 and 23. Why is having a single focus more natural for someone who treasures God?

- Ask someone you trust to suggest what weights you need to lay aside. Don't answer that person immediately. Think about what he or she has said.

- What would help you pay more attention to your life: journaling, meeting with someone regularly to confess sins and pray together, taking communion weekly or daily?

- Consider how you respond to the idea of God longing for us. What does that idea make you want to pray?

QUESTIONS FOR DISCUSSION AND REFLECTION

1. What stood out most to you in this chapter? Why?

2. In what areas do you live on automatic pilot? Do you sense any call to simplicity in these areas?

3. Which benefit of simplicity do you need most: tranquility, integration, relating to people and nature, or authenticity? Why?

4. What does this chapter lead you to want to pray?

5. Which of the above experiments do you see yourself trying out this week? How might you tweak them to fit you better?

WHAT SIMPLICITY MIGHT LOOK LIKE

~&~

AT THE BEGINNING OF CHAPTER THREE, I suggested that we need to be intentional by making plans to rearrange our lives in a way that makes more space for God. Chapters four through nine present specific disciplines of simplicity in which you will be invited to do that rearranging of your thinking and experiment with certain ways of speaking and doing.

If you view these next six chapters and the suggested experiments at the end as adventures, that will help you. Rely on God's grace to empower you and the Holy Spirit's wisdom to nudge you to try some of these things (even if they seem odd), and lean on God during the experience. Don't judge the outcomes too harshly but pay great attention to the inward conversations. You may want to record your thoughts in a simplicity journal or reflect with a friend about what you're hearing from God about yourself and your journey of trust.

Please feel free to modify the practices. The guideline for all spiritual practices is a version of Benedictine John Chapman's words: "Pray as you can, not as you can't." This means focus on a simplicity practice as you can do it, however imperfectly, not as others do it or the supposed one right way to do it. If you find yourself overwhelmed in a certain chapter, go on to the next one. Try to address that overwhelming chapter later and see what happens then. Your part is to do the connecting (through the disciplines), and God's part is to do the perfecting.

Most of all, keep your eyes on God as the treasure. Know that union with God is what you were created for, and you can taste it here and now. Have courage and enjoy.

4

FEWNESS AND FULLNESS
OF WORDS

Let no evil talk come out of your mouths,
but only what is useful for building up,
as there is need, so that your words
may give grace to those who hear.

Ephesians 4:29

WHAT TWO TERMS WOULD others use to describe the words you speak? Helpful but plentiful? Witty but self-focused? What adjectives would you *like* for people to use to describe your speech? Peaceful and supportive? Truthful and insightful? It was said of Quaker founder George Fox that "the fewness and fullness of his words have often struck even strangers with admiration."

William Penn went on to talk about how Fox was "no busy-body" and "it was a pleasure to be in his company." Not only did Fox speak little, but when he spoke, his carefully chosen words welled up from a single-focused heart, creating a clear and compelling effect. It was obvious to others that he treasured both God and them.

Speaking concisely can be powerful, as we see from Fox's life. Words that are few in number but deep in fullness rise up from a heart that has examined and distilled its motives and given up trying to push itself forward or win over others.

I saw this one night several years ago when I took part in a support group for parents of teens. Our leader had urged us to think about what we'd say when we confronted our teenage children so we could be calm and clear. Sometimes we even rehearsed with the group. As one father explained what he planned to say to his son, I could see his intense desire to get through.

First, he would list what his son was doing that was inappropriate: coming in late, not doing his homework and skipping school. Then in a more positive spirit, he would inspire him with free use of Grandma's car if he received B's or better on his report card. Finally, he would close with a list of drop-dead consequences, such as no computer or cell phone, if his son's behavior didn't improve. And if none of these tactics worked, he had a little quip from a police sergeant to toss in: "Skipping school is the first step to a life of crime." Satisfied, this dad exhaled, smiled at us and relaxed his shoulders.

I was impressed with his three points and the zinger until I remembered our group leader's frequent comment that teens hear only ten percent of what you say, so start saying ten percent of what you usually say. That same week I'd delivered bad news to my then-teenage daughter in a short statement. I made no elaborate facial expressions, and I held my hands at my side, not on my hips—I can't tell you how hard that was! Then I gently kissed her on the top of her head and quietly walked away. My new motto, "Say it short," worked better than all my years of explaining myself. She simply complied. But I sympathized with the father in our group. Like him, I'd learned to impress and persuade people by presenting my ideas with snazzy flair.

My journey in simplifying speech began back then, and this less-is-more approach helped me see that I was using words to convince colleagues to do what I wanted them to do and to impress friends with what I knew. I realized that my wordiness revealed a lack of trust that God would work without help from me.

I found that simplicity and gentleness of speech—using fewer words and speaking slowly—made it more likely that my words would "impart grace to the hearers" (Eph 4:29 NKJV). I could inwardly feel that speaking in this succinct, straightforward manner was developing patience and kindness in me as I limited my efforts and relied on the Lord to shepherd me in each situation. To my surprise, people also heard me better. They thought I actually meant what I said because I said so little.

Yes and No

While communication is important, talking has its limits. It doesn't work if our goal is to express ourselves rather than create space for God's grace to flow. If we feel we have to convince friends, coworkers or spouses in order to get our point across—by using capital letters and emoticons in email, for example—we're losing sight of the fact that God can provide the security we need without our going into overdrive. When we feel overlooked or slighted, we're especially tempted to exaggerate or "overspeak," such as saying we love something when we only like it. Jesus' instruction sounds radical to a world that routinely communicates in bold print: "Simply let your 'Yes' be 'Yes,' and your 'No,' 'No'" (Mt 5:37 NIV).

This simple yes-or-no way of speaking was the opposite of the "evasive swearing" common in Jesus' day. Good Jews could swear by something other than God (heaven, the earth, Jerusalem or their own head) but have no intention of following through (Mt 5:33-36). As long as they didn't swear by God's name, they could vow anything impressive-sounding without obligation. As a result, they served two masters: honesty and sincerity but also manipulation served up with empty promises.

Even though I've made enormous progress from the time I was in that parents of teens support group, I recently read a statement in Franciscan Richard Rohr's book *Everything Belongs* that describes what's going on inside me when I try too hard: "Faith does not need to push the river because faith is able to trust that there is a river. It is flowing. We are in it." Rohr connects this "river" to the Spirit, according to Jesus' words in the Gospel of John: "'Out of the believer's heart shall flow rivers of living water.' Now he said this about the Spirit, which believers in him were to receive" (Jn 7:38-39).

"Faith does not need to push the river."

Richard Rohr

I read this a few months before a speaking engagement I did regularly where I tended to push the river because I particularly loved this group and its instructor. I wanted to do well. Yet I'd noticed that my instructor friend often didn't look at me when I was leading. Was I distracting because I was trying too hard? I sensed Jesus inviting me: "If you are thirsty, Jan, come to me. If you trust me, drink. Don't push the river—let the river of the Spirit flow out of you. I will do this. Don't try too hard. Relax in me."

I meditated on this idea for weeks and when the day came, I was able to rest in God. In worldly terms, my first presentation was a "hit." The second, however, was not. The participants didn't engage as they had in the first session, and they told me they felt like they'd disappointed me. But I gently replied that none of this was about me; the Spirit would work in ways none of us understood. We needed to trust that. And this time, my friend in charge had not looked away. I left sensing that God had ministered to people and that I had learned a great deal about not pushing the river with my words.

Taking Our Words to Heart

After Jesus told his followers to let their yes be yes and their no be no, he added a PS: "Anything beyond this comes from the evil one" (Mt 5:37 NIV). Is this an overstatement, or are lips truly, as Dallas Willard says, "the main thoroughfare of evil in human life"? Not only can we injure others with our words but we feed our self-indulgence when we use them to get our way. Here's what I wrote in my journal when I first began engaging in inward conversations with God about my speech:

> Slowing down my speech and pausing to hear what goes on in my mind shows me that I've used words to make sure I'm noticed or well thought of. I'm shocked at how hard I work at making people like me or getting them to look up to me. Sometimes I don't detect all these motives within, but later I know I did something wrong because I feel sad in my relationship with you, O God. You must grieve that I don't trust you with other people's opinions of me. So often you could have used me to love the person in front of me but I was too busy trying to look good with my words. I don't like that. I want to live knowing you delight in me, and that really is enough.

At this point, I better understood what Thomas à Kempis wrote in *The Imitation of Christ*: "Many a time I wish that I had held my peace. Why, indeed, do we converse and gossip among ourselves when we so seldom part without a troubled conscience? . . . We often talk vainly and to no purpose; for this external pleasure effectively bars inward and divine consolation." As I realized that chatter crowds out inward conversation with God, I began surrendering two major habits.

Convincing others. We may not pressure someone at the point of a gun, but we do it with the point of our words, because words—think of talk radio, websites, TV advertisements, campaign speeches—are what persuade people. We often push with our words because we think we're right, but people can't hear our point when our voice is drained of love (Eph 4:15). In these instances, our heart has stopped trusting God to work.

Christian witnessing in particular can become pushy. Consider that witnesses in court simply report what they see. They don't have to convince anyone. So in witnessing about our faith we tell what we see and experience with God. In fact, being "quick to listen and slow to speak" is especially powerful in conversations about God because it sets up an atmosphere of listening, which helps the other person become more likely to hear the nudges of the Holy Spirit (Jas 1:19). *Our listening* to them makes them more likely to *listen* to the Spirit.

Such a witness is full of authenticity instead of affectation. Wise Francis de Sales, a French bishop who wrote about spiritual direction and spiritual formation, said, "Simplicity, meekness and modesty are always to be preferred. Some people never make a gesture or movement without so much affectation that everybody is annoyed by it. . . . Those who affect an artificial manner and do nothing in a natural way are very disagreeable in society. There is always a sort of presumption in such people. Ordinarily moderate cheerfulness should predominate in our associations with others."

Like William Penn describing George Fox, de Sales describes a person who is down-to-earth and relational, without pretense of any kind. Both Penn and de Sales mention how pleasurable it is to be in the company of such a genuine person who is not self-conscious or calculating.

Impression management. Aiming for simplicity in speech helps us be straightforward without posturing. We are the same person in every situation. We always act in character, never working behind a mask. Without simplicity, we may try too hard to make an impression when meeting new people or choose to defend ourselves when it's not necessary.

A few years ago I joined a group that met regularly. When I introduced myself, I stayed within the suggested three minutes and managed not to engage in my old game of "Say something that will make everyone laugh!" or "Say something so deep or authentic-sounding that people will be impressed!" But I began noticing that others exceeded the time limit, and I became resentful that they got more attention. Clearly, I had a lot of room for progress.

Yet as I learned to introduce myself without fanfare, I saw that I built relationships more naturally. I saw that in the past I had misled people into thinking I was more than I was—more clever, more witty or more spiritual. Then I had to live up to that or risk disappointing them. Simple was easier.

Impression management is a form of insincerity, even duplicity: what you see is not what you get when you know the real me. At times, impression management is even about trying too hard to seem sincere—we feel we must explain our sincerity at length. Such a life is exhausting because we're working against what is real. We lack tranquility and authenticity. In fact, one way we can tell we're engaging in impression management is the loss of a sense of peace within. When that happens, we need to ask ourselves what we're up to.

Perhaps you're thinking that energetic and artful speech or talkativeness doesn't always arise from self-preoccupation.

Aren't some people just witty or friendly? Yes, but these gifts from God can be well used to impart grace to others instead of drawing attention to ourselves (Eph 4:29). Indeed when Samuel Johnson was asked the purpose of conversation, he replied that it was to "promote kindness."

Conversely, enslavement to talking causes us to habitually say what pops into our head without considering whether our words serve others. We tend to be especially self-indulgent and long-winded with family members and close friends, rattling on about a missed appointment or near-miss traffic incident. We forget that our intention—what we really want—is to bless the ones we love.

Moving Toward the Heart of Christ

Simplicity of speech flows from a heart that has bonded with the heart of Jesus: compassionate and truthful, loving and good. But because we're only moving in that direction and have not yet arrived, our words reveal other things that are stored in our hearts: "For out of the overflow of the heart the mouth speaks. The good man brings good things out of the good stored up in him, and the evil man brings evil things out of the evil stored up in him" (Mt 12:34-35 NIV). If we are putting our confidence in ourselves instead of God, this shows in the force and volume of our words. Comments "just slip out" because they've been home-steading in our hearts for years.

> Our words reveal other things that are stored in our hearts.

When we first become aware of this reality, our mouth feels as if it can't help itself. Just try to stop interrupting other people's speech if that's what you normally do. Try not to raise your voice if you feel no one is hearing you. When I began my say-it-short experiments with my teenagers, I often caught myself two sentences into a "Mom speech" before I stopped midsentence and left the room. Then I collected myself: What small thing do I need to say but nothing else? What feelings in me would be better left unexpressed?

Such searching of the heart helps develop an inward simplicity of thoughts and longings. Our mind becomes less cluttered with destructive motives, as Richard Foster describes: "Speech becomes truthful and honest. The lust for status and position is gone because we no longer need status and position." As our journey of trusting God grows, our mouth can state an idea briefly and peacefully and then allow others full freedom to respond.

At one point I felt so utterly unable to offer intentional, grace-filled words that I barely spoke at all. That missed the point; I still wasn't imparting grace to the hearer. So in the midst of conversations I began asking God, "How can I draw others out instead of talking about myself so much? How can I promote kindness?" Indeed, the real battle is what goes on in our minds as we converse. Instead of thinking of what we want to say, we work at silencing our thoughts and becoming fully present to the other person.

Speech Therapy

Certain practices allow the Holy Spirit to retrain our hearts, minds, mouths and gesturing hands in simplicity of speech. They cultivate confidence that God will manage our reputation and not let us be walked on or ignored. Here are a few practices to consider.

Silence. Personal or group silent retreats help us see how content we can be when we're quiet, although at first it can be very uncomfortable. The effects of silence spill over into a quieter way of being in conversations.

As an experiment for a class, my graduate student Peggy explained to her family that she would be silent from late Friday evening until church on Saturday evening. Here are a few of her reflections:

> I couldn't speak, so I had to express myself through actions. I saw that I shouldn't always rely on words to tell my family how much I love them. It's my actions that make the difference.
>
> My family seemed happier to have my attention. My words weren't as important to them as my attention. Once when my husband got off the phone with my son, I could see he was mad but I couldn't say anything. I could only comfort him by touching him. And it worked better!
>
> Since I wasn't filling up the room with my voice, my family was able to say what they wanted to say to me. My son especially enjoyed this and talked to me a lot more. (Maybe if I'd just be quiet, he'd open up more.)
>
> I see I need to stop telling people what to do. I was surprised that my family made it through the day without my reminders or complaints about getting things done. Things did get done; and if they didn't, it didn't matter. I learned that God is the one I need to talk to about everything—even what to do next.

In Peggy's twenty-four-hour experiment with silence, her daily conversation with God grew, and she was able to love her family in ways that met their needs better than her speech had. She experienced a taste of the abundant life here and now that humans are created for.

Situational silences. We may choose to be silent in short, specific circumstances that otherwise send us into overdrive. One such situational silence that is particularly formative is attempting not to have the last word—i.e., not adding the last zinger or comment that begins with, "Just for the record . . . "

or "I just wanted you to know . . . " or "I don't want you to think
. . . " This practice helps us "have nothing to do with stupid and
senseless controversies; you know that they breed quarrels" (2
Tim 2:23). It forces us to trust God with the outcome.

Another kind of situational silence is to try not to give your
opinion unless asked. At first I found this downright painful.
People expressed their opinions but didn't ask for mine! I felt as
if my arm or leg was being amputated because I was unable to
announce the deep insights I'd spent years developing. Often I
turned around, walked away and wailed to God (who I'm sure
was laughing), "How will they
know how brilliant I am unless I
express myself?" Later I would
ask him, "Why am I so worried
about what others think?" Then
finally I would surrender and
pray, "O God! I want all my dependency needs to be centered in
you. Help me do that!"

> "It is a wholesome act of
> humility to withhold the
> expression of our opinions."
> *Shirley Hughson*

Shirley Hughson, a well-known spiritual director from the
past, wrote:

> It is a wholesome act of humility to withhold the expres-
> sion of our opinions, at least until others have spoken, or
> until we are asked to give our judgment. Often when we
> have accurate knowledge of a subject which is being dis-
> cussed, it is a real act of mortification to refrain from
> speaking; and this constitutes the exercise of humility.
>
> One of the most frequent and hurtful occasions of pride
> is the readiness with which most of us give our opinion, or
> instruct others, on any subject that might be introduced
> into a conversation. A wholesome exercise of humility is to
> yield our opinion without hesitation unless we are sure that

in such yielding some fundamental truth will suffer. We are
not called upon to correct all the inaccuracies of others.

Confession. It helps to admit to God and perhaps to someone
else our missteps when we indulge in showy speech or talk
about ourselves. In this process, we also ask God to show us the
fearfulness and neediness behind our words: Does this person
intimidate me? Do I remember a time they've been unkind?
After we've done so, we need to speak aloud God's forgiveness
of us with a statement such as, "In the name of Jesus Christ, I
am forgiven." We can then ask God to help us plan the next
step, which is often a spiritual practice. One friend puts her
hand over her mouth when she wants to interrupt. That small
effort is powerful for her.

Welcoming the stranger. When I first began to practice simplicity of speech, I gave up small talk because it seemed self-
focused and inane. But then I realized this warmup dialogue
with people we meet for the first time or don't usually discuss
deep issues with is a way to welcome a stranger (Mt 25:35;
10:40-42; Jn 13:20). By offering a sense of home to others (Jn
14:23), we become inviting and hospitable toward people we
don't know well or who might feel uncomfortable. Small talk
can be a vehicle of grace, such as noticing that someone's blue
shirt brings out the beautiful color of their eyes or asking for an
update about a concern they previously spoke about.

N. T. Wright tells about a time he was invited to lunch by a
friend who had invited twenty or thirty other people as well.
Nearly all of the guests were well-known public figures, used to
having the conversation revolve around themselves. The situation had the potential to become fiercely competitive. How
would these people interact?

After saying grace, the host said, "Remember: the most interesting person in the room is the one you're sitting next to." His comment, no doubt, gracefully nudged his guests toward attentive listening to one another. I have often thought of this comment while interacting with people at conferences, and it has helped me invite others into conversation—to promote kindness.

Grace for Yourself

If you decide to experiment with simplicity of speech, please understand that you're in deep water because the tongue lives on autopilot. Expect to fail, and when you do, don't beat yourself up. Reflect on your motives and invite God to speak to you. That inward conversation is what will transform you, so don't be discouraged. We do this practice "as we can, not as we can't." And we're grateful that the Holy Spirit empowers us to do it at all. Ask God to show you what you would be like in conversation if you felt secure and content with God's own self as your treasure.

The ideas in this and subsequent chapters are merely experiments. You may wish to try some of these disciplines of abstinence for a week, a few days or a few hours. Even then, keep listening. For example, I decided to eliminate telling people I was praying for them because I sensed I was trying to appear spiritual. This practice of the discipline of secrecy allowed me to pray in secret (Mt 6:5-6). But now and then I sensed that it might be helpful for someone to know I was praying. So now on occasion I tell the person. This may seem a little slippery, but the important issue is learning to sense God's nudges versus our self-indulgent habits.

If we make even an inch of progress, the rewards are enormous: not being so self-absorbed, seeing into the hearts of others more easily, being able to hear the prompting of the Holy Spirit because we're less chaotic inside. This is the rich way of dwelling in the kingdom of God

EXPERIMENTS WITH
SIMPLICITY OF SPEECH

- Write, think or talk with a friend about the two words you would like to be used to describe your speech. Pray for that.

- Try not to speak at all for a certain period of time. This might be a day or morning or just an hour of solitude away from pressures and demands. You might hike or go to an art gallery, browse in a favorite bookstore or walk across a bridge that has always fascinated you.

- Plan your next foray into small talk—at the bus stop, for example, or during greeting time at church. How might you welcome a stranger but not indulge yourself in talk that is not helpful and necessary?

- Pray to become the kind of person whose talk demonstrates the Spirit's power instead of clever eloquence (1 Cor 2:2-5).

- Ask God as you begin each day this week to help you love and respect others through simple, helpful speech. Consider the people you'll see whom you're likely to "run over" with words—to convince them of something, because they routinely run over you, or because they love you so much they let you run over them. You might think about this in the shower or as you tie your shoes.

- Conduct a three-, ten- or thirty-day experiment with abstaining from a speech practice, such as interrupting others or yelling at a rude driver, and replacing it with a grin or the words "Bless you." Pay attention to what goes on inside you immediately afterward.

- Try to answer a question today with a simple yes or no. Listen to what happens inside.

- Think about who you are most likely to interrupt. Why is that? How might you pray for that person now when he or she isn't in front of you?

- For one week, do not give your opinion unless asked, give advice unless asked or have the last word in a discussion.

QUESTIONS FOR DISCUSSION AND REFLECTION

1. To what person, group of people or kind of person would you most like to impart grace? What might that look like?

2. What is the difference between being shy or reserved and practicing simplicity of speech as described above?

3. What feelings or situations are most likely to get you talking more than is helpful or necessary? What do you need to know from God in those moments?

4. What does this chapter lead you to want to pray? Be specific.

5. Which of the above experiments do you see yourself trying out this week?

5

LIVING LIGHT IN
A LAND OF PLENTY

*And God is able to provide you with every
blessing in abundance, so that by
always having enough of everything,
you may share abundantly in every good work.*

2 Corinthians 9:8

BEFORE THE BORTHWICKS met and married, both Paul and
Christie had decided they didn't want to be squeezed into
the world's mold by pursuing a consumption-oriented lifestyle. So they made certain choices to that end. For example,
Christie decided to take her lunch to work so she could save
hundreds of dollars each year that could be used to pay
someone's annual tuition in a country such as Chad or
Uganda. As a couple, Paul and Christie asked themselves a
question before making any major purchase: "What else
could we do with that money?"

A few decades into their marriage, a house sitter complained
that their house was "the most technologically out-of-date

house I've ever stayed in." Their furniture was old, their cars used, and the bathroom was original to the house. They had no DVD player. For years they hadn't even had cable, and when they did get it, half of the channels were incompatible with their twenty-year-old television set.

On the one hand, they felt embarrassed that their friend had been uncomfortable in their home. On the other hand, they felt a silent sense of intentionality. They were content with their choices. They believed they not only had enough but were rich. Says Paul Borthwick, author of *Simplify: 106 Ways to Uncomplicate Your Life*, "It's easy to compare ourselves to neighbors or even Bill Gates, but if we think globally, we're in the top five percent of the world's wealthiest people."

Making that decision years ago to downscale the American dream has meant that the Borthwicks live to the beat of a different drummer. As a result, they're free to say yes to God in ways that others might not be able to do. In 1998, Paul was on staff at a large church and had a good salary and excellent benefits. "But it became clear the Lord was directing us to venture out," he says. "We were in our midforties, when people begin to think about security. But because of our choices in the first twenty years of our marriage, we were free to go out (as Abraham is described in Hebrews 11:8) 'not knowing where [we were] going.'"

Their venture took them into a combination of teaching, international mission work and leadership development, and they've never made the same salary since. "Years of living a simpler lifestyle gave us the freedom to be liberated from golden handcuffs," Paul says. "We had low house payments and no car payments. Our secure salary tempted us to stay in that comfort zone, but what God had for us was outside that box." And they have loved life outside the box.

The Borthwicks understand that they are the "rich in this present world" (1 Tim 6:17 NIV), globally speaking, because their income is far more than $7,000 a year, the worldwide average. (Consider how low some incomes must be to be averaged with higher U.S. figures and still come out to be $7,000.) This understanding has helped them practice frugality, a discipline of simplicity in which we limit the possessions we choose to both own (this chapter) and acquire (chapter six).

This pruning work of eliminating even some good things is radical in a culture that routinely says, "The sky's the limit" and "If I can afford it, I must deserve it!" Our living spaces are often cluttered with too many objects and our vacations hurried with too many good things to do. Jesus, however, knew the deep goodness of limiting oneself. Though he was in the form of God, he limited himself by being born in human likeness so that he could offer the ultimate gift of love. He saw great value in limiting his daily activities so that he did without food, others' praise and ill-gotten power (Phil 2:6-8; Mt 4:4-10).

Sensible, Grateful Stewardship

To practice frugality is to refrain from owning things we don't need or using money or goods to gratify a hunger for status, glamour or luxury. While some people don't own certain luxuries because they can't afford them, those learning frugality limit their possessions as a matter of principle. So a rich person might choose to live frugally, and many have.

Practicing frugality is especially important for those of us who live in industrialized nations. To cope with plenty as we live in the land of plenty means to refrain from excess. We keep only what we truly need, use and can manage well.

Frugality as it relates to simplicity of life does not always mean owning less or spending less. For example, says Paul

Borthwick, "My wife and I could have one car and it would cost us less, but it would complicate our life rather than simplify it."

While frugality might mean penny-pinching, stinginess or bargain-hunting to some people, the word means something different for followers of Christ. Lutheran scholar James Nash explains, "Its Latin root, *frux*, conveys the essential character of frugality: fruitfulness and joyfulness! It finds joy in justice and fullness in restraint. Frugality connotes moderation, thrift, cost-effectiveness, and satisfaction with material sufficiency—similar to the 'contentment' described in the first Pauline letter to Timothy (6:6-10)." Consider those phrases again: joy in justice, fullness in restraint. That's what abiding in Christ is like. It's abundant.

Though extremely practical, frugality is also deeply spiritual. It trains us to put our trust in the One who is unseen and eternal, to be good stewards of what is seen and temporarily entrusted to us by God and to be generous and willing to share (2 Cor 4:18; 1 Pet 4:10; 1 Tim 6:18). To practice frugality is to begin to believe that the most real stuff of life is never what we own; it's our interaction with a living God with whom we partner to bless others.

Practicing frugality does not give us something extra to do but guides decisions we already make. As we shed excess possessions, we have more time and energy to spend on things we deem important: hanging out with God, paying attention to people and serving in adventurous ways that previously took a back seat. It becomes easier to share money and possessions with joy. As followers of Christ, we commit ourselves to continually raising our standard of loving rather than our standard of living.

Practicing frugality forms character by helping us learn hu-

> Practicing frugality forms character by helping us learn humility.

mility. As it trains us to be satisfied when our unnecessary desires are not gratified, it curbs self-indulgence so we don't always have to have our way. We become more content and grateful, relishing and managing well what we have rather than resenting what is missing.

How Much Is Enough?

For most people, "enough" is always a little bit more than what they now have. That's why even those with plenty have to learn to be content (Phil 4:11-12). According to research published in the book *Your Money or Your Life*, increasing income creates a curve of fulfillment. When people finally have enough to survive (as many in Third World countries struggle to do), they begin to experience a sense of fulfillment. The curve starts at the bottom of the chart and moves upward. As they acquire a few comforts, their sense of fulfillment increases and the curve continues upward. The curve rises again with the addition of luxuries. Then it peaks. As more luxuries are added, the curve starts downward. Additional luxuries continue to deplete the sense of fulfillment and the curve plunges back to the bottom.

When people have more than they need, they're weighed down, distracted and distressed. They may even become enslaved to paying things off. This process illustrates the scriptural truth that self-indulgence breeds distraction and stress (Lk 8:14; 1 Tim 6:9). It may seem to ease stress at first, but this is an illusion. Acquiring and owning more than we need actually wears us out (Prov 23:4).

The presence of discontentment and even depression among the rich casts doubt on the idea that making more money will satisfy us, says Robert Lane, professor emeritus of political science at Yale University and author of *The Loss of Happiness in*

Market Democracies. Lane describes how, despite the fact that people in prosperous democracies find their wealth satisfying, many are also haunted by a spirit of unhappiness. His research shows that once people's earnings rise above the poverty level, an even larger income contributes almost nothing to happiness.

Acquiring and owning more than we need actually wears us out (Prov 23:4).

Their main sources of well-being are friendships and a good family life, not possessions. In fact, increased prosperity often has a negative effect: as wealth increases, family and community erode, and individuals become more distrustful of each other. This makes sense when you consider that often in prosperity we become more self-indulgent. That makes us more self-centered and difficult for others to deal with, and so relationships suffer.

Dissatisfaction increases when what we own owns us. Possessions enslave us, requiring our time and money to clean, maintain and store. Consider the supposed blessing of a big home. "Americans have apparently run out of room, even though the average house now has 2,330 square feet, up 55 percent from 1970. . . . The insatiable race for space is fueling a $15 billion self-storage industry." Bigger homes require more time and effort to clean, furnish and maintain. Fewer people are renting carpet shampooers, snow blowers or bench saws but owning them instead so that everything is ready at their fingertips. Robert C. Roberts, professor of ethics at Baylor University, concludes, "'Upward mobility' often ends not in satisfaction and peace, but in exhaustion, disappointment and emptiness."

Contrast these feelings of exhaustion, disappointment and emptiness with the Borthwicks' excitement and adventure in being able to come alongside Christian leaders in the under-resourced world as encouragers and teachers. Their personal freedom from financial burdens allowed them to say yes to God to be concerned for others and to affect the world.

The Distraction of Too Much

Frugality is particularly difficult but especially important these days because accumulating more than we need is normal. Teine (pronounced "Dana") Kenney, a certified professional organizer who helps people "exorcise" their home of unused kitchen appliances and clothes they no longer wear, estimates that about eighty percent of the U.S. population struggles with owning too much. "If you were at a store and there was a blue triangle on the forehead of every person struggling with clutter, you would see people up and down the aisles with blue triangles."

Kenney helps us understand why we own more than we need. "People find happiness in possessions because they're trying to fill the empty hole in their souls with physical things. It's an indication of a bankruptcy of the spirit." In fact, she continues, when clearing out extraneous possessions, "people experience a scraping as if they were having a surgical procedure done. Excess possessions become these persons' outward identity." Their stuff is who they are.

Kenney offers as an example a woman who has worn size fourteen clothes for ten years but still has her size two clothes from college. When Kenney suggests getting rid of the size two clothes, she becomes angry. "She hurts inside," Kenney says. "She fears giving away those clothes even though they're just a collection of molecules."

We have to choose between our stuff and our serenity because physical clutter creates mental clutter. "There is no escape from the toll that [stuff] takes on your life," says Don Aslett, founder and owner of a cleaning company. "Everything stashed away or hidden discreetly is also stashed away in your mind and is subconsciously draining your mental energy. Why spend a valuable part of yourself polishing, washing, dusting, and thinking about [stuff]? You can't afford [it]. It will rob you physically, emotionally, and spiritually." Perhaps this explains why we become tired at night but are unable to rest.

"Everything stashed away . . . is also stashed away in your mind."

Don Aslett

Decluttering our living space makes it easier to declutter our life because our thought processes are no longer clogged. Practicing frugality reinforces intentionality, prodding us to continually ask ourselves, *What do I want?* and *What do I really need?* Our heart also gets cleaned out, a process that creates the opportunity for many inward conversations with God.

What's Behind Our Stuff?

As you read the following, have an open heart regarding any tendencies that may be affecting you more than you realize. If you attempt some of the experiments at the end of this chapter, watch especially for these inclinations to surface and be ready to work through them.

Longing for importance. Some people find a sense of significance in possessions such as their home or car. They are unaware of this feeling until it's suggested that they sell that item.

Longing for love. Owning possessions is sometimes our substitute for a sense of being cared for as children. Objects may represent the attention we didn't receive.

Fear of not having enough. People save things to provide a false sense of security—if they accumulate enough, maybe they'll never run out! This is particularly true for some who grew up experiencing scarcity or poverty.

Guilt and regret. Kenney notes, "In people's garages, we find unopened wedding gifts and items they never use but can't give away because they'd feel guilty if they did. Or stacked on people's desktops are things that cause regret—invitations they forgot or theater performances they didn't go to. They saved these things because they thought they should have gone. They're afraid to be the master of their own time. So we work on learning to make decisions on the front end such as deciding how many events they'll go to each month so they don't have to feel guilty about turning things down."

Guilt and regret are usually accompanied by a fear of making decisions. "Clutter is usually the result of delayed decisions which really are decisions—to do nothing," Kenney continues. "It's important to learn to make definite decisions and live with results of that decision." Delayed decisions are often about fear of making wrong choices.

Perfectionism. Most of us have heard the suggestion, "If you haven't used it for a year or more, get rid of it." I have done that several times, but here's a confession: When I go looking for that absolutely perfect shirt to go with something, it's gone. A part of me laments giving it away! I've been learning to laugh and say to myself, *So you don't have the one perfect shirt in the universe, girl! You will be OK.*

Inability to accept where I am in life and who I am. Kenney tells of a client who had been an esteemed teacher: "She had thirty years of curriculum in her garage. When she retired, she saved it for teachers who said they wanted to go through it, but no one came to do that. We had to sit with her and help her see who she was now. 'How do you intend to live?' we asked her. She had grandchildren and a husband to take care of. So we urged her to pick out two bins of curriculum to use with her grandchildren. It took her a while to be quiet and realize, *That's who I was but not who I am now. I was a good schoolteacher and now am a good teacher to my grandchildren.*"

Some people struggle to make decisions and articulate preferences because they don't know themselves well enough to know if certain things fit with who they are. That's why we need to explore those central questions of life: What do I want? What do I long for? So Kenney helps people do this: "We help clients slow down, be still, and see they are wonderfully made creatures with distinct likes and dislikes. For example, some people have all sorts of eclectic, incongruent artwork or styles of clothes or home decorations. When we explore why, we find out some things were gifts or they bought what someone else liked or they bought it while they were lonely and watching the shopping channel. But when we find their preferences, a congruency emerges and then they do the work about not feeling guilty about getting rid of things they don't like and never use." That question "What do you want?" remains central.

This may be a moment for you to slow down and be still. Quietly look at the list above. Ask God to show you in the next few days what you need to know about what you accumulate and why. If you become aware of these motives and feelings in the next few days, present them to God and perhaps to a wise friend to discuss how to work through them. If these motives and feelings are not examined, no amount of clearing out will help.

When God Becomes Enough

Think about the kind of person you want to be. Maybe you want to be more patient, more open to listening to others and noticing their needs, or not so irritated at all there is to do. Frugality helps with this. For example, people often say they wish they were more patient. Limiting what we own builds patience as we get used to thinking, *I don't have to have what I want right now.* It helps us pay attention to others because we're not so preoccupied with our possessions—making sure everything we own is absolutely "presentable" (which really means impressive and better than it normally is). There's more space to treasure God because we don't go to sleep thinking about the backyard swing that didn't get cleaned or the items we need to purchase tomorrow in endless errand running.

Perhaps you wish this chapter included more how-to ideas. Numerous books, websites and organizations are available to help you with that. My goal has been different. I want to invite you to consider the beauty of limiting your possessions so you can have space to treasure God. I also hope to assist you in looking within at fears and finding freedom from enslavement to what seems normal.

Consider the experiments below prayerfully. If they're too much, trim them down to size. Ask God to help you fine-tune them and to suggest to you experiments that fit you exactly. Your goal is not to be more frugal. Your goal is to bond more deeply with God as you disengage from the possessions around you.

∽

EXPERIMENTS WITH
FRUGALITY OF OWNERSHIP

- Pray this prayer often enough that it becomes the way you think: "God, of your goodness, give me yourself, for you are enough for me" (Julian of Norwich).

- If something of value is being distributed in a group—fish at the end of a fishing trip or leftover food at a picnic—take nothing and see how it feels. In fact, give away your portion and notice what happens within you. Beware, however, of that proud do-gooder feeling. Can you just do it and ask God to bless the others who took the items?

- Walk through your house or apartment. Try to find ten things that don't belong there: the coat that is too small, the antique that is too precious to use, the boxes you've never unpacked from the last time you moved. Collect them and look for opportunities to give these items away or to donate them.

- Take a personal retreat in a place that is sparsely populated, barely furnished and maybe even barren in the landscape. When you return, look around and think about what you'd like to get rid of.

- Make a decision about how much closet space you want to devote to clothes or how many bookshelves or cabinets to garage or kitchen items. Work toward possessing only that amount.

- When you think about buying a tool, book or piece of clothing, consider what tool, book or clothing you already own that you would then give away.

- Pray this prayer, "God, O God, break the tyranny of created things," every time you (pick one):

    can't find something

    rest your eyes on a pile of stuff

    notice a luxury you could easily do without

QUESTIONS FOR DISCUSSION AND REFLECTION

1. What possession do you own (or have you owned) that seems to own you?

2. What aspect of frugality surprises you most?

- Globally speaking, you are rich.
- It's not owning things just because you can afford to buy them.
- It's not bargain hunting.
- It's about stewardship and good management of God's gifts.
- It forms your character with humility, contentment and gratefulness.
- Other:

3. What, if anything, keeps you from feeling you have enough?

4. What does this chapter lead you to want to pray?

5. Which of the above experiments do you see yourself trying out this week?

6

A GENEROUS,
NOT GRASPING, LIFE

*Command those who are rich in this present
world not to be arrogant nor to put
their hope in wealth, which is so uncertain,
but to put their hope in God, who richly
provides us with everything
for our enjoyment. Command them to do good,
to be rich in good deeds, and to be generous
and willing to share. In this way
they will lay up treasure for themselves
as a firm foundation for the coming age,
so that they may take hold of the life that is truly life.*

1 Tim 6:17-19 NIV

THE GROUP PARTICIPATING in the retreat I was leading always began by "laying the altar." One at a time, each participant laid on the center table an object that represented that person's experience of God that year. Tabitha dangled a pronged object over the table's corner. At the end of each prong was a figure of a person dangling. She said it showed how she had given up

control that year. Even though I'm trinket-phobic, I was mesmerized by the object. It illustrated a major theme of my life:
my ongoing surrender of control to God. In the back of my
mind a voice said, *I must have one of those! It's for my spiritual
life, right?*

Instead of paying attention to these people I came to serve, I
began thinking about where I might buy such a thing. Suddenly
I felt tired just thinking about visiting knickknack stores. That
brought me back to reality and I thought, *You don't need a thing!
Enjoy watching it this weekend.* So I looked at it and thanked
God for helping me learn to surrender. As time passed, I became mildly horrified at how quickly I—a very frugal person—
had begun thinking, *I must have it!*

Practicing frugality involves two changes: limiting what we
already own (continually clearing out our possessions and giving them away), and limiting what we acquire (buying more
possessions, hours spent shopping). Such limiting of self flies
in the face of a culture where shopping is such a favorite pas-
time that even people who aren't planning to buy anything
want to look at things through the windows. It's not just fe-
males who do this. I recently trailed behind a male relative
walking through a warehouse-size hardware store and watched
him pick up an item every ten feet to ogle over.

Frugality does not always mean spending less or finding bar-
gains but also focuses on limiting what we acquire to that which
benefits others and teaches us to rely on God. For example, if
we buy fair-trade coffee as a simple way to benefit Third World
coffee growers, we may spend more than we would on regular
coffee but benefit people in the process. (Fair-trade coffee growers earn a living wage, which provides the opportunity for a
better quality of life.)

The frugal person operates with intentionality, discernment

and clarity of mind, analyzing expenditures by asking, *Do I really need this?* With wisdom frugality says, "Give me neither poverty nor riches, feed me with the food that I need" (Prov 30:8). The vigilance of frugality spawns lively conversations with God in place of the simple question, *Can I afford this?* It cultivates generosity of heart so that we become people who continually wonder, *How might I benefit others?*

Frivolous Consumption: Corruption of the Soul

Consumerism is an attachment to materialistic values or possessions because we think they're required for our happiness. Unfortunately, followers of Christ are not exempt, as observed by Evy McDonald, a minister and cofounder of the New Road Map Foundation, a nonprofit organization that helps people align their values with their spending habits:

> A theology of consumption [has begun] to invade our culture—and our churches. Slowly, almost imperceptively, we['ve] wandered away from the foundational teachings of Jesus—sharing our wealth, identifying with the marginalized, living a life of grateful stewardship—and [have begun] to identify our worth with how much money we made or how many possessions we owned. . . . Our identity has changed: from being American citizens to being American consumers. We now produce very little for ourselves. We have become voracious consumers of not only goods but services, all in an attempt to increase our quality of life.

Opportunities to shop abound, from Internet websites to print catalogs, from the home shopping channel to shopping malls (which outnumber high schools).

Prosperity is not wrong, but routinely spoiling ourselves is—getting what we want whether or not it's wise. The Jerusalem church leader James told the rich to weep not because they were rich but because they had indulged themselves "in luxury, satisfying your every desire" (Jas 5:5 NLT). No matter how much or little we earn or own, self-indulgence damages our character. Dallas Willard says, "The spiritually wise person has always known that frivolous consumption corrupts the soul away from trust in, worship of, and service to God."

We've wandered away from the foundational teachings of Jesus.

If this idea of soul corruption sounds too harsh, medieval or otherwise weird, you might think of it like the stealthy, slow decay of a tooth. A tooth is a beautiful invention by God that helps us chew nourishing food, and it gives us an inviting smile. But undetected decay eats away at the enamel of the beautiful tooth, into the dentin and finally to the nerve. If we make daily choices to limit contact with decay-producing matter by brushing our teeth, the tooth might just hold up for life. But if not, the tooth is slowly corrupted until a two- or three-surface cavity develops and requires a crown or even removal. Each little choice of self-indulgence corrupts us a little more every day.

Self-indulgence corrupts the soul because it trains us not to be satisfied unless we get what we want, which lays the groundwork for greed to grow. This disordered desire for wealth seems harmless when we fantasize about winning a lottery or finally making it rich, but ethics professor Robert C. Roberts helps us see the consequences:

Our culture is little inclined to see greed as a major source of human troubles . . . [but] greed can create the anxiety, depression, and loss of meaning that often comes in middle age after a "successful" life of acquiring the "goods" of this world. Greedy people seek out stimulations that arouse and titillate their acquisition fantasies, just as lustful people seek out stimulations that arouse them sexually. If lust finds certain frustrated gratification in perusing the pages of *Playboy* or *Playgirl*, greed finds similar satisfaction in ogling stylish clothes, computers, furniture, and kitchen appliances.

If the comparison with lust seems too strong, consider that both harbor the same feeling: *I must have it now!* Does coming across just the right outfit, power tool or computer gadget make you want to grab it immediately? I confess to seeing the right blouse and thinking, *Now that would make me look shockingly good!* That's a feeling of enslavement.

Because self-indulgence is a character issue, Ron Sider, professor of theology, holistic ministry and public policy at Palmer Theological Seminary in Wynnewood, Pennsylvania, insists that every budget is a moral document. A personal budget that lists my planned expenditures reflects what I value, and a national budget reflects what we as represented by the government value. Is all the money spent to take care of me or the nation, or is there space to help others—especially those in need?

To get a picture of greed on a global scale, imagine yourself at a round table set with five plates. Then imagine five people seated at the table. One person owns or controls four of the plates, but you and three others huddle in front of one plate, sharing it. How do you feel about the person who owns four plates? I did this in a class with five students and five paper plates. The look on the faces of those four who together held one plate—very good Christian college students—was venomous.

That eighty-percent-versus-twenty-percent ratio is real. Well-developed countries such as the United States, Europe and Japan (roughly twenty percent of the world's population) own or control four of the "plates" (eighty percent of the world's economy). The remaining eighty percent of the people in the world are left with one "plate" (twenty percent of the resources). This analogy helps us understand why so many people in the world lack food, shelter or any kind of health care while a relative few of us live in increasing luxury. On average, one American consumes as much energy as two Japanese, six Mexicans, thirteen Chinese, thirty-one Indians, one hundred twenty-eight Bangladeshis, three hundred seven Tanzanians or three hundred seventy Ethiopians.

Such a comparison invites Christians in developed countries to consider how we as the "rich in this present world" might "do good" instead of consume more (1 Tim 6:17-19 NIV). How can we live more simply—not using eighty percent of the world's goods—so that others may simply live? Writer and theologian James A. Nash explained, "The moral problem is not mainly that we seek 'bad things' . . . [but] too much of the many good things in life. . . . The prosperous people of the planet are guilty of greed and gluttony, two of the seven deadly, or primary, sins. The two are usually partners in producing excess." As the "rich in this world," we need to learn to live with limits, both moral

How can we live more simply so that others may simply live?

and physical. This will benefit other people—as well as plants, animals and the cosmos—but it will also enrich our own character toward Christlikeness. It moves us toward that union with God we were created for here and now.

Heart Exam Issues

While self-indulgence deceives us into thinking we need things we only want, practicing frugality brings clarity. It helps us distinguish between necessities and luxuries. It trains us to withstand the desire to indulge ourselves, breaking the world's domination over us as we intentionally limit spending and manage resources to help others. Through frugal actions we say, "I want to live at the need level, not the greed level."

But the power to buy things, especially if we haven't ever had them before, can be heady. So once more we need a heart exam: What is it within me that feels the need to be self-indulgent? What feelings and issues drive my purchases—inadequacy (fear of not being a good enough parent), the desire to impress (wanting to appear younger than I am), people-pleasing (making sure I do exactly what people ask of me) or perfectionism (having just the right purse or high-performance rims for your car's tires)?

Here are some of the supposed payoffs of consumption that entice us into self-indulgent living.

Achieving goals. Peter Walsh, author of *Enough Already! Clearing Mental Clutter to Become the Best You*, explains, "We buy things, but we also invest in 'the promise.' We buy exercise machines, but we are really investing in the promise of flat abs. We buy clothing, but we are really investing it in the promise of being more attractive. We buy all that stuff from late-night infomercials, but we are really investing in the idea that somehow our lives will be better and our homes will be happier." Buying a gym membership or enrolling in a diet program feels like an accomplishment in and of itself, as if we're halfway to the goal of losing weight.

If we feel we must buy things to achieve goals, we become enslaved to making money. Extensive shopping steals time and energy from the rest of our life and makes unrestrained use of credit cards obligatory. A minister tells about asking a successful

Christian businessman why his heart was not as warm toward the things of God as it had been. "'Business has been dominating my life,' he admitted, then added in defense, 'but I'm not seeking it. I'm just trying to handle what's coming in. What do you expect me to do?' I suggested he could say, 'Enough is enough.' He looked at me as if I were insane. The desire for more had a greater pull on this man than his desire to follow Christ, use his spiritual gifts, serve his wife, or be a father to his kids."

Feelings of importance. Certain purchases have social value and convey a desirable image. This desire for importance breeds in us a passion for the latest and greatest. In chapter three I mentioned laying aside the "weight" of being up to date (Heb 12:1). Buying a new car, a new phone or new shoes strokes the ego and provides a false sense of security or self-esteem. This usually originates in a sense of not feeling loved or valued, a deeper problem that purchases cannot heal.

Love of novelty tends to condemn a thing simply because it is old and to desire a thing simply because it is new. Whatever is newer or faster must be better, so we go out and buy the latest gadget or most recent version of a video game. In fact, if we own something that is not the latest, people look at us in disdain.

Long after others had switched to high-speed Internet service, I kept dial-up for quite a while. I felt my needs were met at that time, so why switch? During a telephone conversation one day, my colleague sent me an email to scan but when I told him I had to wait for the modem to connect, he said in disdain, "I can't believe you still have dial-up!" I laughed. My friend had grown up in a very poor country, but now that he lived in America he had little patience for anything less than the latest.

Allaying fears. Fear of passing up a "good deal" is actually a fear of missing out—a fear that betrays us and keeps us from living intentionally. We need to remember that as long as there are malls, flea markets and Internet shopping, there will always be another bargain.

Pain management. We often use shopping and spending to cover up unwanted feelings of sadness that result from, for example, making mistakes at work or failing as a parent. Hence this saying has become popular: "When the going gets tough, the tough go shopping." If shopping becomes an all-out addiction, spending can actually take the place of feeling.

Relieving restlessness and boredom. Some purchases arouse emotions we desire. For example, purchasing a horror novel may stimulate feelings of adventure and excitement. Buying perfume may stimulate feelings of romance. We often shop to escape the routine.

While God created us with a sense of adventure, we often reduce this God-given sense to a craving for nonstop variety. But variety, another "weight," as we discussed previously, creates mental distress—making so many choices is exhausting. Next time you're in a supermarket, stop at the chip aisle or cereal aisle (now they fill aisles!) and count the choices. Is all this variety good for us? Do we really need to spend this much emotional energy choosing cereal or potato chips? It's soul-corrupting in the sense that it teaches us to devote time and energy to things that have almost no value compared to treasuring God and being involved in what God is doing.

A life with God is full of true drama. We participate in others' lives in an authentic way and are exposed to stories that genuinely move us. We are presented with challenges and risks that stretch us. The Borthwicks, if you recall, knew the real adventure of moving out of a comfortable position to live on faith. They were able to do this because they weren't encumbered with many expenses. I think that because they did not involve themselves in the pseudodrama of purchasing and

Life with God is full
of drama.

owning lots of things, the real drama of living in the kingdom of God and making an enormous difference in people's lives was more obvious and appealing to them.

Discernment Experiments

To discern if any of these supposed payoffs are misleading you, try this experiment the next time you shop: As soon as you consider buying something, become mindful of your body. Does your pulse speed up a little? Do you experience a surge of adrenaline as you check out? Does your mouth feel dry or watery? Then listen to your mind. What reasons are you giving yourself for buying this item? *It's for someone else; it's on sale; I've looked everywhere for this thing!* Then explore what's behind those thoughts. Perhaps you'll find, *I'm a clever shopper—watch me!* or *I make good money and I deserve to spend it,* or *My life is empty and I deserve this.* Write down these thoughts as soon as you can. Looking at them on paper gives us a stone-cold realization of what we live for and what drives us.

Try to let this process be about you and the formation (or corruption) of your soul rather than the item itself. At times this exercise has made me laugh and walk away from the item. At other times I haven't been able to tell what's going on inside so I tell myself, *Set down the item. If you really want it, come back after getting what you really came to buy.* Usually I forget all about it and don't regret walking away. At still other times, the exercise has scared me a little because I've seen that the item represents goals of self-importance or fears of inadequacy: *I'm the youngest person on the teaching staff. I must buy this to wear so I don't look like a kid.* In those times I confess I haven't been able to complete the heart exam. Sometimes I've bought the item, but many times I've run out of the store, chanting, *What I've got is fine!* Admittedly, this *Just flee!* option is not the best, but we practice this discipline as we can, not as we can't. I'm confident that fleeing is better than reinforcing a slight corruption of my soul. In fact, it follows William James's advice to deny ourselves a little something each day.

Here are some other experiments.

Try asking God about a purchase. Richard Foster explains, "When you decide that it is right for you to purchase a particular item, see if God will not bring it to you without your having to buy it." Foster tells the story of a friend who needed gloves for work and prayed about it instead of rushing out to buy them. In a few days someone gave him a pair of gloves. Foster explains, "The point is not that he was unable to buy the gloves; he could have done that quite easily. But he wanted to learn how to pray in ways that might release money for other purposes." Such prayer not only reduces impulse buying but also teaches us to trust more deeply that the Lord really is our shepherd and provides everything we need.

Try waiting. Since disciplines of abstinence are often about pausing, try waiting before you buy something. When I was first married and my husband and I had little money, we paged through catalogs when visiting my husband's parents and plotted how soon we could afford certain things. My father-in-law teased us, saying, "Wait a year and see if you still want it." He was right. If we waited, we forgot about that thing or figured out it wasn't the best thing to buy or we wanted something else more.

One version of this type of delay is the thirty-day list. Write down what you need with the assumption that if you still need or want it after thirty days, you'll buy it then. In those thirty days, you'll have to make do with what you have, which not only teaches trust and humility but can also be fun and inspire creativity. While I was helping my niece move, we considered renting a dolly to move filing cabinets into and around her house. I asked if they had a sturdy skateboard, which is what my son uses as a dolly. No, they didn't, but another niece grabbed her little girl's toy shopping cart. We were careful with it, but you wouldn't believe the heavy things we moved with that toy and how we laughed about it. We thoroughly enjoyed this mini-adventure of making do.

Borrow before you buy. If a desired purchase is hobby-related, distinguish serious sustained interest from curiosity about current fads. This especially applies to sports and fitness equipment. Borrowing an item for a while can help you figure out if you'll use it. Consider that the average Exercycle is used 7.2 times and then retired.

Freedom to Give

Frugality's corresponding engagement discipline is generosity. If a raise in salary doesn't automatically signal the purchase of a flat-screen TV, it could cause us to ask God, *In light of what you've been teaching me, how might I use these additional resources to raise my standard of loving instead of my standard of living? What do you wish me to do with this money based on the adventures you've been leading me into lately?*

Sharon illustrates how being around people in great need spurred both frugality and generosity. "We wanted to give more, but the pressure to maintain our standard of living was comprehensive. While praying with the International Justice Mission country director for the work in Guatemala, my husband was especially touched by the self-centeredness of our resource allocation. How could we own such a large home when others had little or nothing? Clearly others had significantly greater basic needs. Our house was already on the market as a result of our earlier decision to simplify, but very little was sell-ing at the time. That night Bob prayed a prayer of faith, asking God to sell our house so we could use our collected resources to help others in need. The next day our buyers saw the house for the first time!" As Sharon described in chapter one, this downsizing meant she and her husband could buy a smaller house for themselves as well as hold a loan for a Congolese immigrant family they'd gotten to know.

Limiting purchases can help us learn to live a generous life instead of a grasping life. Nestled among Jesus' teaching about loving enemies and not judging others is this: "Give to everyone who begs from you; and if anyone takes away your goods, do not ask for them again. Do to others as you would have them do to you" (Lk 6:30-31). This entire passage is about giving and forgiving freely instead of acting from self-interest. The more we fall in love with God, the more we understand that God is "generous . . . to a fault: he provides good things for all to enjoy, the undeserving as well as the deserving. He is astonishingly merciful." This God whom we treasure will lead us into an astonishingly generous, merciful life.

ॐ

EXPERIMENTS WITH
FRUGALITY (ACQUISITION)

- Try not using your credit card for something you can't afford. Experiment with maintaining a sense of rightness about living within your means. God has provided what you need.

- Deprogram yourself from advertisements by not listening to the radio in the car.

- Thank God for something old that is still serviceable.

- Pick a few items you intend to use until they wear out. Figure out what "worn out" would mean—holes in the elbows, three times repaired, and so on.

- Next time you need something, look for it at a thrift store.

- Limit window shopping or catalog shopping for a month. How does this affect your thoughts and desires—do you feel deprived or cheated? Even if you don't throw away the catalog but only set it aside, this can be progress.

- Pray to live at the need level, not the greed level.

- Write down, ponder or talk with a friend about the last thing you bought that you didn't plan to buy. Did it turn out to be a wise purchase? How do you feel about it now?

EXPERIMENTS WITH GENEROSITY

- Investigate companies that are committed to social responsibility and helping others, such as fair-trade coffee producers. Consider purchasing the more expensive product because you want to help others.

- If you save money through frugality practices, donate that money to a cause or person you have prayed for and care about.

- Consider how you might use the power of your wealth to help others. For example, shop at a smaller neighborhood store that employs low-income kids.

- Meditate on 1 Timothy 6:17-19 and imagine what it would look like for you to be "rich in good deeds" and how that would enable you to "take hold of the life that is truly life."

- Look at the things you have. Who might need one of those things? How do you feel about giving one of these things away? Try it.

QUESTIONS FOR DISCUSSION
AND REFLECTION

1. What sort of things make you think, *I must have this!*

2. How is self-indulgence a character issue? Give some examples.

3. Which of the payoffs of consumption listed above have you already worked through? Which one, if any, do you need to pray about?

4. If you had more resources at your disposal, to what cause or person or project would you give more?

5. Which of the above experiments do you see yourself trying out this week?

7

THE INTENTIONAL, UNHURRIED LIFE

Careful planning puts you ahead in the long run;
hurry and scurry puts you further behind.

Proverbs 21:5 *The Message*

AS PEOPLE CATCH A VISION of treasuring God and being transformed into Christlikeness, they often say, "I wish I had more time to . . .

- not live such a rushed, hurried life so I could be more aware of God."

- *be* with people—be less concerned about getting them to do things to make my programs successful."

- volunteer with a certain cause or situation because that's where I think God is nudging me."

- get a real sense of what Jesus was like, perhaps by reading the Gospels more."

- just be with God—to hang out with God."

If you started a list of "Things I Wish I Had More Time to

Do," what would be on it? Making such a list is an act of intentionality. Simplicity of time involves focusing in on what we really want, what we long for.

Getting More Done

Contrast that mindset with the normal cultural emphasis on managing time for the sake of efficiency and productivity. The goal of our society is to pack as much into one day as we can, as if quantity created quality. We are what we accomplish, so that chaotic schedules impart a momentum that seems to be lifegiving. Checking off all those weekend chores makes us feel important. Adrenaline becomes our drug of choice. In our busyness we become addicted to fulfillment, which leaves "little time for love to make its home in us," as spiritual director Gerald May used to say.

Who or what exactly pushes us? It's usually our drive to achieve and our desire to squeeze every ounce of worth out of something. After I'd written and taught a college course, I was asked to teach it again. All that initial writing and planning had not resulted in a good hourly income rate, so I figured teaching it the second time would be so much easier that I'd make up for it. So I agreed, even though it crowded my life to a suffocating point. In trying to get my "money's worth" out of my first effort, I struggled to love and be attentive to my students the second time. My supposedly time-wise, money-wise choice was stressful and not people-wise or love-wise. It hurt to realize this because it had been years since I'd done such a thing.

Simplicity with time requires the diligent intentionality of creating enough space that I may say yes to God about treasuring God and loving people.

At other times nonstop activity, whether paid or volunteer, helps us avoid spending time with a spouse we don't enjoy, children we don't understand or acquaintances who drag us down. Maintaining a hectic life can be a way of avoiding larger issues such as guilt or bitterness from the past, disappointment with how our life is turning out, or the work that needs to be done in relationships that confuse or frustrate us.

Motives: Busyness Is Next to Godliness

The heart exam question in arranging our time is, *What's running me?* An early step in living intentionally in the companionship of God is to figure out the ideas that drive us: *I want people to value me and look up to me; I must get certain things done by the age of thirty-five or forty-five or fifty-five.* Consider the things we do to impress people, such as being "the helper" or "the one who knows stuff" or the "go-to guy": "I'm the guy they consult when . . . ," "I'm the one who writes movie reviews for the local paper" or "I'm the one people on our street call in an emergency." We may dislike that this role takes up so much time, but we like the role itself. Ego and pride keep the pressure on.

> The heart exam question about arranging our time is, *What's running me?*

Anytime we take on a role, we depart from the simplicity of being who we are: nothing more and nothing less. Living up to a role moves us into the duplicity of insincerity instead of the authenticity of transparency, which is valued in the kingdom of God (Lk 12:2-3).

Other times we are enslaved to busyness out of fear of being left out or of offending people we like. Then our choices are forced, not intentional. If we're asked to do something we don't want to do—going to a wedding of someone we don't know well, going shopping with a spouse—but have told ourselves, "I really should go," it's wise to pause.

If you find you don't really want to do something, sit with

that thought and ask God to help you explore it. Too many followers of Christ beat themselves up when they don't want to do something they think they should do. Then they force themselves to do it out of guilt, which often leads to resentment. When they do this, they miss an exquisite opportunity to have a conversation with God.

So next time that happens, try asking yourself what I've come to designate as "the Holy Spirit question": *What is this really about?* We have to be very quiet when we do this and know God is with us in a most grace-filled way. Then we can see ourselves more clearly, understanding that we perhaps agreed because we:

- want to be loved and valued by others

- want to be considered a nice person

- have to show up at gatherings if we're going to have any friends

- are too embarrassed to admit we're exhausted and need to rest

Learning discernment helps us. It's good to ask ourselves, *What am I called to do today or this weekend to love God and let God's love for me overflow to others?* Stay as open as you can. God might be loving and nurturing you—as well as stretching you—to take more Sabbath, to read a book that requires you to think hard, to nudge you to visit relatives you haven't seen for twenty years, to serve on a team that visits people in prison, to attend an activity where there's someone you can't stand so you can experiment with loving your "enemy" (anyone you find difficult). Sometimes we'll get this wrong, but that's not the worst thing that can happen. We'll still grow in discernment, which is both a gift and a skill. We learn to be motivated by God, not other people's good opinions.

Making Space: Living an Unhurried Life

God's idea of Sabbath keeps us from living like wound-up toys. "In recovering the Sabbath, we begin to turn away from the mad consumerism that destroys our souls and the environment," writes Ron Sider, founder and president of Evangelicals for Social Action. "Sabbath gives us time to rest our tired psyches, enjoy our families and neighbors, and take delight in the presence of our God—in short, helping us treasure the truly spiritual, and become people who treasure holy leisure over the opportunity to accomplish one more important task, or build another balcony in our Tower of Babel."

The divine rhythm of Sabbath is built into creation as God rested on the seventh day (Gen 2:3). God rested not out of fatigue or tiredness or to be recharged to work some more but because it's a good idea. We were built for times of hard work and outward expression (engagement) but also quiet hiddenness (abstinence). We must have them both. Crops grow better with a Sabbath; animals labor better with a Sabbath. To pause and know that God is God is wisdom. Jesus protested not the Sabbath itself but the way it had been systemized and suffocated so that a person was forbidden to do good (Mt 12:12; see also Deut 22:3; Prov 3:27).

Practicing Sabbath regularly in some form keeps us from heading into a two-week vacation knowing we'll need a full week to wind down before we can enjoy it. That means we've been wound tightly for a long time. When we arrange our time intentionally and loosely, we need less time to wind all the way down.

On Sabbath we turn loose of the world and stop trying to make things happen, which transforms our character into being more God-dependent and less controlling. Our time to "cease

from action" (that's what "rested" means in Genesis 2:3) may
look different from another person's; it doesn't work to be legal-
istic about it. Sabbath was made

We've been wound tightly
for a long time.

for us, to help us (Mk 2:27); we
weren't made to fit woodenly into
it. Sabbath can be a forty-day retreat, a full day every week, a
morning or a half-hour at a time—especially in the beginning.

Margins

The more we practice Sabbath, the more likely we are to live an
unhurried life, leaving margins of time in our days. The apostle
Paul understood how we need this: "I want you to have all the
time you need to make this offering in your own way. I don't
want anything forced or hurried at the last minute" (2 Cor 9:5
The Message). And the more we have pauses of unscheduled
time in life, the better Sabbath works.

When I first began practicing Sabbath years ago, a wise friend
advised me that I would also need moments of "serious nothing" sometime during the week. Because she knew I was catch-
ing planes and speaking, she predicted I wouldn't be able to
move at a hundred miles per hour and then stop on a dime for
Sabbath. Her phrase "serious nothing" was so much fun to say
aloud that I would laugh and say to myself, "Now for a little
time of serious nothing." This slowed me down.

Studying Jesus' healings shows us that he must have had
plenty of margin in his days because so many of the people he
healed interrupted him as he was on his way somewhere else.
I'm sure I would have been the impatient disciple standing next
to him thinking, *I so wanted to get to Capernaum by sundown!*
Would these healings have occurred if he hadn't had space, if
he'd been in a hurry? Jesus knew that "one who moves too hurriedly misses the way" (Prov 19:2).

If we knew that the most important things we ever did would occur as a result of interruptions, how might we live differently?

Consider what it would look like to allow time to reflect after reading Internet news or the newspaper. You might ponder, *What were the causes behind these events? What does this tell me about our culture? How might God be leading me to pray?* A life of Sabbath, pauses and margins creates a stillness inside us that infuses each thought and conversation. Others pick it up and enjoy being around us.

Lisa talks about her efforts to keep "white space" on the family calendar:

> My husband, Colin, a computer programmer, was taught to use 'white space' (tabs, spaces, blank lines) in his code to make it more readable for other programmers. Early in our married life he let me know he needed more 'white space.' I accused him of wanting to stifle me.
>
> Finally we read the book *Margin* by Dr. Richard Swenson and I could see that God was bringing to my attention my frazzled, burning-the-candle-at-both-ends way of life! We began putting on the family calendar one entire weekend per month with no obligations. We also set this boundary: never four consecutive nights out.
>
> Now years later, I love our planned white space because God uses that time in such creative ways. We don't rush from event to event; I'm not frantically baking or preparing for the next thing on top of trying to be a Christlike wife and mother. Instead we play more together, we have a peaceful home to hang out in, and we enjoy our intentional commitments because we've also spent time at home with each other.

Lisa and her family refuse to live beyond their means socially, with too many social events, lunches out, work-related activities or kids' activities. Other people I know have set boundaries within their days such as limiting television and shutting down the computer by nine p.m. Such boundaries are practical statements of intentionality: This is what I will and will not do. This is the "careful planning [that] puts you ahead in the long run" (Prov 21:5 *The Message*).

Making Choices: Intentionality of Time

In general, arranging time intentionally involves certain thought processes, but first, consider this story.

Paula Huston was a college instructor who began enjoying the direction of a mentor-monk-friend, Father Michael, at a nearby retreat center. First he instructed her about Sabbath, and she began doing odd things like having her first massage—so many knotted muscles were discovered in her body that the kind-hearted masseuse had to work around them. After she'd experimented with various creative ways of "resting," Father Michael told her, "I want you to write down every single responsibility and duty in your life. Obligations that are so important you simply can't get out of them." So she listed sixty-two extremely important items. Then her mentor-monk-friend told her to cross out half of the things. That took her three weeks. She says:

> Cutting that list in half . . . was downright bracing. . . . At first I trembled . . . then I grew increasingly ruthless. "Item fifteen," I'd say, tapping my teeth with a pencil. Hmmm— that wickedly humorous, two-page, single-spaced Christmas letter I send out to three hundred of our closest friends each year. Can I really give it up? Won't people be puzzled? Or even hurt? . . . Off to the dumpster, item fifteen.

Huston withdrew from committees, skipped readings of visiting colleagues, turned down speaking engagements and asked her boss for an extension on a deadline.

This was extremely uncomfortable business for a person like me, old Ms. Reliable. What would my colleagues think? What would happen to my career? I was slowly, deliberately giving up my place in the center of things, my spot in the busy hub. I was disengaging for no apparent reason, walking away from new challenges.

Huston suffered the disapproval of some of her colleagues, which triggered her own self-doubt. But she continued her Sabbath experiments and went on to say yes to God through an early desire to write short stories. She concluded that previously her work had defined her; after this process, she had a life.

Processes That Help

Many books and seminars offer steps for prioritizing activities. Richard Foster suggests this simple approach to simplifying one's schedule: List everything you do for one month. Then rank each thing you did: (1) essential, (2) important but not essential, (3) helpful but not necessary, (4) other. Once you have your list, ruthlessly eliminate all of the last two categories and twenty percent of the first two.

To arrange our time so intentionally helps us let go of many good things. The first time I did an exercise like this I gave up leading an innovative group at church that I had started. No one could believe I was doing this, but I found it gave me space to be a more relaxed mother. God invites us to stop moving through life sleepwalking with all our decisions on cruise-control and to be intentional in what we do.

When you're pondering what activities must stay or go, it

helps to have first done the work we've described earlier. So at the top of whatever list you make, write your answers to: *What do I want? What am I longing for? How is God inviting me to say yes in this season of life?* If you're worried about offloading a certain time commitment, trust that God will prompt another person to take it up.

At some point you'll probably need to list your regular current activities. When you do, be ruthlessly honest so that you know "what is." Include every run to Starbucks, weekly neighborhood chat or Saturday football game with the guys. As you classify activities as essential, important and so on, see how they fit with what you really want and with what you need. That Starbucks run may actually be Sabbath or some form of renewal or just plain fun (the discipline of celebration). The more clearly you connect activities with intentions, the more you'll discern how your current rhythm of life can be modified.

Expect to be challenged as your motives reveal themselves. What happens inside you when you consider eliminating or abbreviating certain things? Who are you trying to please or win over? What are you trying to avoid? For example, that daily Starbucks might be trimmed to three times a week, or maybe it's altogether out of the question at this point in your life. Maybe running errands only once a week would help you confront that self-indulgent, I-must-have-it-now feeling. Or not. Do this as you can, not as you can't. You may sense you need to let God woo you away from guys' night out or having your nails done, but at the moment this activity means too much to you. Can you put it on the table for discussion with God? To think, *I may be willing to be convinced* is enormous progress for some.

When you're done making your list of what you do, consider what is missing. Is there space to breathe? Is there substantive community life where you can say what you really need to say?

Are there practices on your list that help God satisfy the deep longings of your heart? If not, do you need different practices? Who might help you discern these?

If your season of life has recently changed, you might experiment with radical changes. For example, when my kids started attending high school, I quit all my weeknight evening commitments so I could drive them to their activities. My husband was a bivocational pastor and I was beginning to speak on weekends, so I decided that I was totally theirs on weeknights for this season. People complained that they missed me, so I told them what time to meet me at what coffee shop but explained that I'd have to leave at a certain time to pick up a kid.

At first it seemed like a sacrifice but then I saw how beautiful it was. First, I found that I was relieved to have a legitimate excuse to quit all these things. (This says a lot about motives. I was doing what was expected by others or for my career, but they were not things I was authentically called to do.) Next, it put me in the car with a teen or two who sometimes found it easier to say certain things to me in the privacy of darkness when they knew I couldn't look at them. And I found I enjoyed my one-on-one meetings with people at coffee shops. They could be their real selves rather than whomever they'd brought to all those groups I'd belonged to.

Of course people scolded me and told me my life was "out of balance." But it felt so right that I didn't defend myself. I did, however, feel the weight of all that running around and started taking a weekly Sabbath.

Be careful of giving balance too big a place (especially others' opinion of balance). This assumes life divides itself into even categories—fifty-fifty, as we say. Your life won't always flow into even categories, and it's artifical to try to make that happen. God works through relationship and guidance. When Ecclesiastes 3 talks about times to plant and uproot, to tear down and to build, it's not talking about percentages but about a sense of rightness and calling. Each of us in our friendship with God grows in discernment of what we are being drawn toward. We learn to live in this sense of peace to the point where we recognize it as soon as we're out of kilter and we've lost it.

Now here are some cautions.

This process often backfires if we don't first work through the question *What do I want?* and then *Why do I want that?* The "why" question explores our hidden motives for what we do. Heart exam work is essential; it's as important as any schedule change we make.

If the final result doesn't include some kind of Sabbath and margin in your life, what you've done will probably amount to rearranging chairs on the Titanic. The ship will still go down.

Move slowly. This process may take you several days or weeks or months. Don't attack it in high-efficiency mode. Work with patience and generous humor. Expect to find some comical absurdities in your life. Approach it as a conversation with God in which God reveals to you where you've been headed and what you'll have to do to aim for an interactive life with the Trinity. Just take the next step, whatever that is.

As with all spiritual practices, do it as you can, not as you can't. My experience is that people hold on to certain activities even after working through the above process. As they continue through life, however, they realize, *I'm done. I'm grateful I did this, but I'm done.* Then they let go of it. Gradually, loving Christ "decides everything."

Serving from the Deepest Place

One of the greatest struggles people face when considering simplicity of time is their service commitments. If you're challenged in this area, focus all your efforts on considering what you want—what you really want—and ask yourself, *What breaks my heart that breaks the heart of God? What tugs deeply at me?* In the classic book *A Testament of Devotion,* Quaker pastor and college professor Thomas Kelly talked about this process: "The Loving Presence does not burden us equally with all things, but considerately puts upon each of us just a few central tasks, as emphatic responsibilities. For each of us these special undertakings are our share in the joyous burdens of love. . . . We cannot die on every cross, nor are we expected to." Narrowing our focus to our inner calling is what the apostle Paul did by reaching out to Gentiles. No doubt he received criticism for focusing on Gentiles since he had the equivalent of a Ph.D. in Judaism.

For example, I was serving in numerous areas and feeling burnt out when I began asking myself what broke my heart that broke God's heart.

> "We cannot die on every cross, nor are we expected to."
> *Thomas Kelly*

The other avenues of service were interesting and fun (and they made me look good), but they weren't "the place where your deep gladness and the world's deep hunger meet." When preparing to speak on Matthew 25:31-46 about Christ being among the hungry and thirsty, I felt such a longing to serve with the homeless that I put down what I was doing and began calling local agencies. After several calls, I found out that a drop-in center for the homeless was forming. Although the time of day I decided to volunteer was inconvenient and I have had to watch many clients die over the years, I have continued to serve there because I have a deep sense of calling. I know I belong there. It's where I experience Jesus and get stretched beyond myself.

Serving according to calling keeps us self-forgetful (the larger calling of helping the poor is enormous; I just help out) but passionate (working hard, keeping a right heart toward clients). Self-forgetfulness and passion don't usually go together, but serving according to our calling creates that dynamic combination in us as it did in Paul: "Not that I have already obtained this or have already reached the goal [self-forgetful]; but I press on to make it my own, because Christ Jesus has made me his own [passionate]. Beloved, I do not consider that I have made it my own [self-forgetful]; but this one thing I do: forgetting what lies behind and straining forward to what lies ahead, I press on toward the goal for the prize of the heavenly call of God in Christ Jesus [passionate]" (Phil 3:12-13).

As we pursue the things that move us deeply, we let go of mediocre things without noticing. Intentional, prayerful discernment gives us freedom and space to live as God intends us to live.

EXPERIMENTS WITH SIMPLICITY OF TIME

- Practice crabgrass contemplation for a few minutes a few days this week: Go outside, or to a beautiful place indoors, and walk slowly. Don't move forward until you've taken in every color around you. If you wish, touch each texture around you—try rubbing your cheek against it. As you move slowly and do this, listen for every single sound that falls on your ears.

- Start these two lists and add to them as ideas come to you:

  1. I wish I had more time to:

  2. If I did, my next step would be:

- Go for a walk and give God permission to bring up to you the things you do to look important, to appear right or to make a good appearance.

- Try any of the methods in the "Processes That Help" section of this chapter to help you be intentional with your time.

- Consider what Sabbath would look like for you if you began where you are: a slow morning, an hour after lunch to take a nap, permission to have an empty weekend.

- Journal or talk with a friend about what breaks your heart that breaks the heart of God. Ask your friend what seems to touch you that doesn't touch others.

QUESTIONS FOR DISCUSSION AND REFLECTION

1. What stood out most to you in this chapter? Why?

2. What might you joke about being addicted to—eating out, pleasing your boss, finding clothes that make you look shockingly good? How might these activities consume your time and energy?

3. Proverbs 19:2 says, "One who moves too hurriedly misses the way." What progress have you made toward being someone who doesn't do this? What has helped you with this? What is holding you back?

4. What does this chapter lead you to want to pray?

5. Which of the above experiments do you see yourself trying out this week?

8

PUTTING THE "FREE"
IN FREE TIME

∽

So, whether you eat or drink, or whatever you do,
do everything for the glory of God.

1 Corinthians 10:31

THINK OF HOW DIFFERENT IT WOULD BE if our leisure time
were leisurely. What if it didn't involve rushing off to the movie
theater? Not boasting (or moaning) about a busy weekend?
Not having to recover from a hectic vacation we couldn't really
afford?

I confess I was once one of those people who charted out vacation days to make sure we visited every tree and mud hole in the
auto club tour book. Among other things, a statement from Gordon Dahl invited me to change my thinking: "We worship our
work, work at our play, and play at our worship." I was doing all
three. But leisure, I learned, plays itself out best in simplicity.

Free to Choose

Leisure is merely free time away from work and essential do-
mestic activity. For followers of Christ, its purpose is to enjoy

God with all of oneself and to enjoy loving others (Mt 22:37-39). Leisure is good and holy in itself and not just a way to get recharged for a hard-driven, work-only existence or to find relief from a hurried, stress-filled life—as thirty-nine percent of Americans say.

"We worship our work, work at our play, and play at our worship."

Gordon Dahl

Jesus himself enjoyed times of leisure. In fact, he was quite a partygoer, attending dinner gatherings in people's homes and at least one wedding and participating in feast days in Jerusalem. (These celebrations were invented by God for the Israelites. Does it surprise us that God is a party planner?) That two-and-a-half-year camping trip that Jesus and the Twelve took included a lot of work but no doubt quite a bit of horseplay as well.

Jesus also enjoyed beauty, considering a field lily more charming than the best efforts that human beings, including the great King Solomon, could put forth. Reading passages such as Matthew 6:25-34 causes us to imagine that Jesus enjoyed being alive—that, as Tom Wright observes, he often "watched the birds wheeling around, high up on the current of air in the Galilean hills. . . . He had watched a thousand different kinds of flowers growing in the fertile Galilee soil . . . and had held his breath at their fragile beauty."

Leisure time is so important that C. S. Lewis considered it a goal: "The leisure activities of thought, art, literature, conversation are the end, and the preservation and propagation of life merely the means." And also: "Our leisure, even our play, is a matter of serious concern. We can play, as we can eat, to the glory of God." In order to practice leisure to the glory of God and give thanks to God with our bodies, minds and emotions, we need to be deliberate about it and not ignore it or just hope it will happen on its own.

Open Space

Leisure requires breathing space, a pause in activity when we are free from tasks and agendas. When people express concern that spending time in solitude might be boring, I often say, "Think of what it would be like to have a day where you had nothing on your agenda. You could just be." Most people look a little daydreamy and satisfied when I say this, but a few get a look of mild horror on their face. They seem perplexed about how they could possibly endure time not devoted to efficient productivity. To them, an open space of time is not something to be enjoyed but something to be filled up, or even killed, as we say when we're "killing time."

What if, instead, we saw open spaces of time as a fullness of breathing space and unknown opportunity? Having a few hours of open space weekly (Sabbath) sets us up naturally to take small intermissions for "serious nothing" in our days. These pauses create mental space to enjoy God and enjoy others.

Exposure to the natural world creates inward spaciousness. The capacity to slow down and breathe deeply is enhanced by spaciousness of form: beaches on large waterfronts, open skies, rolling hills of grass, wide level spaces in the midst of mountains—even the simplicity of an uncluttered pasture. The unveiling of Jesus' true glory at the Transfiguration could have taken place anywhere, but it seems to have occurred on Mt. Hermon, which is almost ten thousand feet high. It offered broad, beautiful vistas and required an adventurous climb. This meant an overnight stay would have been necessary, which provided the disciples mental space to process the grand event as they hiked back down the mountain.

> Think of what it would be like to have a day where you had nothing on your agenda.

Recreation Energizes

Recreation refreshes, renews and in a sense re-creates the body and the mind. During recreation, we actively participate in something that diverts our thinking and refreshes our attitude: playing basketball, visiting an art gallery, singing in a choir or walking in a park. Active recreation can imitate the adventurous life with God—the excitement of a fast-moving vehicle, the learning of a beautiful yet powerful tennis serve or the harmony of a model train layout that imitates the ups, downs and roundabouts of life but always returns home.

Some people, however, see recreation as a consumer commodity to be used up without reflection, done to gain admiration or grind other people into the ground. It becomes tied up with equipment (a bigger boat, better skis or newer golf clubs) or toys ("He who dies with the most toys wins"). Franciscan priest Richard Rohr notes, "Much recreation does not re-create us, but is only diversionary. I think that's why Americans need so much recreation and entertainment. If it doesn't really entertain or refresh, we will need more very soon. But for open persons, those who know how to receive and let events teach them, a little bit goes a long way."

Consider the difference between playing golf to achieve a good score, to beat a certain opponent or to show off equipment versus playing golf to enjoy the movement of a well-executed swing, to appreciate the beauty of the golf course or to welcome someone new into the family. These latter motivations are about enjoying God—including how God made our bodies to move in ways we didn't know they could—and enjoying people.

Simplicity of leisure involves enjoying the outdoors and viewing natural objects in their own setting rather than as objects that are useful to us: to view a river as a source of beauty and a created wonder rather than a watery surface on which a boat rides to carry water-skiers. This mindset requires a different way of seeing, however.

For example, a large arroyo runs the length of the city where my family lives. As we ride our bikes on the path alongside this arroyo, we have seen all kinds of herons, snow geese, white egrets, cormorants, killdeer, coots, stilts, sandpipers and ducks, as well as more common birds. While hiking in our hills, we've traced the arroyo's headwaters to a nearby mountain pass and wondered at how it makes its journey through our valley and eventually to the ocean. When an acquaintance referred to this portion of God's playground as "the drainage ditch," I didn't know what she was talking about. What we saw as a natural wonder she saw as a place where people might dump stuff.

In light of viewing leisure as arranging space to intentionally enjoy loving God and enjoy loving others, let's look at just a few leisure opportunities.

Travel and Vacation

If we were to stop working at our play, what sort of vacation would be renewing? What do we want? What do we inwardly crave and need?

Vacations of rest. Some phases of life call for vacations of active adventure, and others make us long to slow down. Says Janice, "Our everyday lives are busy raising three teens. Because of hectic schedules, the only vacation that appeals to us is one of rest. We chose long ago to return yearly to a simple cabin on the shore of Lake Michigan, which is large enough to look like an ocean. Our vacation consists of walking the shoreline, sleeping, cooking simple meals and lots of reading, much of which is time spent with God in his presence."

Vacations with a mental purpose. Many people find renewal

in learning vacations where they study archaeology or spend time in founding-fathers environments or examine impressionist painters. The light of God's presence in history and art creates an inner satisfaction that we belong in the wider world and can connect with people we've never met. As thinker and writer Johann von Goethe said, "A person should hear a little music, read a little poetry and see a fine picture every day in order that worldly cares may not obliterate the sense of the beautiful which God has implanted in the human soul."

Some people have taken "roots" vacations to their parents' birthplace in North Carolina or Puerto Rico or the Netherlands. They reflect on what this journey tells them about the people who birthed them and the values they tried to pass on. Knowing more about our own history and viewing the beauty others have created helps us become more self-aware. It can also spur us to treasure God in thankfulness for what we've learned and seen.

Vacations with a spiritual purpose. Other people take pilgrimages to places where special people lived and died or even places where Jesus walked. A pilgrimage involves preparing oneself spiritually and perhaps studying ahead about the person. For example, if you've enjoyed George MacDonald's books, you might read his biography and then visit his home in Huntley, Scotland. On a pilgrimage, you ponder what God might be saying to you as you take in the landscape and architecture. Where is God's presence in this place and how might it have affected this person you admire? Such vacations build in us a groundedness that God is at work on our planet.

To travel as a pilgrim instead of a tourist is to move from a posture that says, "Entertain me" or "Tell me something interesting" to an invitation to experience the Christian journey in a tactile, sensory way, to get us out of our heads. Says Christian

George, author of *Sacred Travels*, about his pilgrimage to the Holy Land, "Having attached personal memories to the biblical sites we visited, the ink of my Bible now bleeds off the page and gets into my bloodstream. It taught me that Christ calls me to surrender my life to him—to take up a cross and walk as a pilgrim and not a tourist."

While teaching in Cambridge, England, I took an afternoon off to take a tour of churches that played a central part in the Protestant Reformation. I began as a tourist and ended as a pilgrim. We saw where people preached and some were martyred, trusting that God was leading them. To climb the spiral stairway and stand in the pulpit where John Wesley preached made me think about how he was so shunned there that he began preaching in the open fields, which led to an enormous spiritual resurgence. At the end of the tour, I sat in the last church structure for a long time and asked God to use me in a fraction of the ways he had used these brothers and sisters who lived before me. These saints whom I'd read about joined my cloud of witnesses, became real to me and inspired me.

Vacations for loving others. Serving vacations give you drastically different experiences from your normal life, allowing you and others to mix fun with physical, mental and aesthetic stimulation when you visit a mission enterprise.

The Painter family spent part of their vacation on a Zuni reservation in New Mexico, where they tutored students, assisted in janitorial projects, programmed computers and wrote grant proposals. Dale, the father, said, "No AAA tour book could have led us into such an intriguing cultural experience." He described being allowed to make the hike up a cliff to a sacred mesa and seeing ancient petroglyphs on the way. This is where "thousands of Zunis fled to escape the conquistadors. Today non-Zunis are forbidden to make this climb unless accompanied by someone from the reservation." Many such mission-oriented vacations offer insider information and moments not usually open to visitors.

Such vacations help us learn skills and meet people we would otherwise miss: learning how to milk a cow when serving on a farm in Appalachia, learning how to farm Amish-style. Computer, gardening and building skills are especially helpful. You need to consider the ages of children or grandchildren and how much of the vacation you want to spend this way.

Vacations that explore. Crosscultural vacations to the developing world will change you for life. Concepts like missions and frugality become personal. You come home with images in your mind of homes made of cardboard walls, kids who share one bed or wires hanging from a ceiling with one light bulb powered by an extension cord stretched from another building or another town. When you hear someone say that God supplies all your needs, you understand that you are a colaborer with God in doing that for others.

> Crosscultural vacations to the developing world change you for life.

Exploring other cultures is more than visiting tourist sites in another country; it's not really leaving home if we go to a developing country and eat at McDonald's. It's about people. If you have a tour guide from that country, get to know the guide and he or she will tell you things you would never find out otherwise.

Taking a vacation where you already know missionaries will help you mix better with the culture and learn more than a tourist ever could. Some people have used their vacations to visit sponsored children overseas in tours organized by child-sponsoring organizations.

These kinds of vacations invite us into simplicity, not only in how they're organized and the worlds they expose us to, but in how they give us a bigger picture of the world God loves and the people in it. We return home thinking it's silly to shop till we drop or think that the latest cell phone is a must-have item.

Drama That Enriches

Entertainment, which is something generally done to or for us, is different from drama, which invites us to enter into human experiences besides our own. Novels, plays and movies as well as performing or listening to music provide mental and emotional inspiration, experiences of joy or celebration, and can create space to enjoy loving God and others.

"It's good to enrich our life with drama, beauty and art in simple ways," says Dallas Willard. "The greatest drama is the cosmos drama, which is the ups and downs of the pursuit of good and its triumph over evil." Drama imparts meaning. People are hungry for drama, which is supposed to come from relationships. "When it doesn't," says Willard, "they seek it as sports fans. So many people grind out their work and they are bored, looking for drama."

God is deeply involved in human drama, entrusting us with many narratives in Scripture, especially in the Old Testament. In the New Testament, Jesus provides drama when he proves to be skilled at street theater and tells stories with surprise endings. By interacting with God daily, we experience the drama of asking, waiting and watching God respond in surprising ways. God provides the drama of our life changing—of us becoming very different people than we were a few years ago, and of our watching other people's lives change.

Because the average American watches more than four hours of television each day, which equals two out of twelve months per year, it's important to be intentional about this activity and to decide what your plan is if you wish to experience simplicity in your time and leisure.

Watching television. You've no doubt heard much about the ill effects of watching television, so I'm going to tell you a story about the benefits of not watching. In my own life, several factors caused me to lay aside the weight of watching TV. I was already upset by how I woke up thinking about murder every morning after watching reruns of *Law and Order.* At that time I also had a spiritual director who didn't watch television. When I'd say, "You know that character on . . ." he never knew. And he had a sense of peace I needed.

But it happened all at once in a period of mental and emotional overload. After being overseas for two weeks (watching no television), I came home to two crises—the death of a close relative and a shocking revelation about another. Processing these events required significant downtime. I sat on our back porch and stared a lot. As I recovered from these things, I still couldn't interface with the chaos of watching television. I found myself out on the porch reading and feeling rejuvenated with a spaciousness of mind. As the days and months and years passed without TV, I didn't miss it at all.

The benefits have been enormous. I talk more to my neighbors, enjoy more sunsets, read more good books and concentrate better on difficult ones. I can clean up my kitchen without rushing. We go to bed earlier and get more sleep. I feel that years have been added to my life.

You may want to experiment with simplicity of leisure by fasting from TV now and then for a week or even just a day. Then do the heart exam we've talked about: What feelings come to you? Before you try it, list what you'll do instead. Get a book from the library you've wanted to read or plot out a gardening project. Figure out what board game you'd love to play with your family but never have time to do.

You can do this in layers. For example, my one exception is watching PBS's *Masterpiece*. We also rent or borrow DVDs from the library but try to choose films featuring a redemptive plot line, taken from a classic novel, offering characters that stimulate us to love and good works or featuring settings and cultures we haven't experienced.

Trust God to woo you into unique practices of simplicity that fit you exactly.

Trust God to woo you into unique practices of simplicity that fit you exactly.

Playing video games. These games provide an interesting experience of drama but often become addictive. Fred says, "My most common simplicity practice is that I 'fast' from all computer games on Sundays until after the evening services. I also abstain from them when I do a Sabbath-style rest, which usually isn't on a Sunday. I think I probably should give up computer games entirely for an extended period because they are too addictive to me."

Eating and Dining

Table fellowship, or eating together around the same table, is an ancient sign of human intimacy that's significant for building relationships. To invite others into this warm space is to welcome them into our life. It honors them because we have thought about the food, either preparing it or choosing a special place to eat out, and decided we want to spend time with that person. It provides a place of peace and also perhaps rousing discussion in which we learn to love by showing interest in each person. A meal is more than something material. It's about sharing pleasure together—commenting on the food itself and celebrating the tastiness of the fruit of God's earth together. Dining together is strategic in loving others and forming community.

The sacramental element of eating together is sublimated, however, when the process becomes complicated: too much food or too much showiness. To keep dining simple is to keep the focus on table fellowship, to be grateful for food and each other.

Once while eating at a restaurant, my friend Sandra prayed a prayer that influenced how I see dining. From a liturgical background, she found "winging it" in prayer a different experience. But looking at our appetizing Cobb salads, she dived in: "Thank you, God, for the people who planted this lettuce. [Pause. I pictured farm workers in the beautiful Salinas Valley made famous by John Steinbeck.] Thank you for the soil and rain that helped it grow. [Pause. I could picture that.] Thank you for the people who picked it. [Pause. I began thinking about how farm workers in California used to use a short-handled scythe, which sometimes cut off hands. So I thanked God for tools and farm labor laws.] Thank you for the people who packaged it. [Pause. I pictured women in packing houses wearing hairnets.] Thank you for the grocer who set it out for someone to buy. [Pause. I thought about our Hispanic produce manager who chose such good-quality produce.] Thank you for the server. [Pause. I reminded myself to find out that young man's name so I could call him by name.] Amen."

When I opened my eyes, the salad looked very different. I saw that a lot of people had served me well. I was thankful. I've since prayed in that manner many times because it reminds me of the simple yet intricate way that food comes to us on our table.

While table fellowship at home is important, it can still seem like a lot of work. I'm grateful that beginning when my children were young, my family was willing to eat simply and didn't crave variety: I fixed double the amount for Monday night and we also ate it on Wednesday night; what I prepared Tuesday night, we also ate Thursday night. And so on.

Now that they're adults, we have family dinner together once a week. We often invite others to join us for these very simple meals. Conversation and games follow. Our goal is to be intentional about being together and enjoying each other as well as welcoming "strangers" by inviting people who probably won't invite us back or who are going through difficult times or who are new to our culture (Mt 25:31-35).

When meeting others for dinner at a restaurant, which is sometimes simpler, we try to choose a quiet place if our goal is conversation and fellowship. (Again we're back to that crucial question: *What do I want?*) Because eating in a home is so laden with relational value, we sometimes order out the food but eat at home.

Simple, Generous Gift-Giving

One way to love God, love others and cut out hours of shopping for birthdays or Christmas is to give a charitable gift selected through a humanitarian agency in the name of the person we usually give gifts to. One organization that offers this service is Alternative Gifts International, which offers gifts from many different organizations at a variety of prices that even children can afford. Now that my kids are adults they give me goats and chickens (supporting microbusinesses in developing countries) but when they were younger, they gave me such things as five dollars' worth of bandages for civilians in Bosnia because all the bandages were being used for the soldiers.

Many churches sponsor alternative gift fairs during the holidays. For example, a church might host a fair-trade store for an evening with the help of a group such as Ten Thousand Villages, which works with over a hundred artisan groups in Asia, Africa, Latin America and the Middle East. The organization sells fair-trade jewelry, home décor and gifts, but best of all they build long-term relationships with artisans that are based on mutual understanding and respect. As a result, these artisans earn a living wage, which provides the opportunity for a better quality of life. People can shop at the event, buying many gifts in one trip that benefit others. This simplifies gift-giving and helps us live a generous instead of grasping life.

My mother was not keen on alternative gifts because they didn't seem personal enough to her, but I sent her a World Vision gift catalog and asked her to give it a try. She gave me a gift of two years' worth of education for two women in Kenya, which was significant coming from her. My mother had worked herself through college going to night school to become a certified public accountant back when women didn't do that sort of thing. This gift turned out to be intensely personal, and I experienced much joy receiving it from her.

Keep in mind that alternative gift-giving isn't a good idea if it somehow communicates to you or others that God is stingy and not bountiful. Indeed, simplicity does not diminish the discipline of celebration: "It is God's gift that all should eat and drink and take pleasure in all their toil" (Eccles 3:13). There are times to spend money on birthdays, weddings and anniversaries and to purchase expensive airfare to rejoice with those who rejoice (or to weep with those who weep). The crucial issue is intentionality: *What am I intending to do? Am I promoting love in human relations or am I being self-indulgent and wanting to impress others? How am I learning to enjoy loving God and loving others?*

ॐ

EXPERIMENTS WITH LEISURE

- Try playing golf or another game—even a board game—without keeping score.

- Talk with someone about how drama enriches your lives. Look for your best examples.

- Plan how much television you'll watch next week.

- Fast from computer games.

- Guard a day so that you have nothing to do. Enjoy. Then talk to God about what that day was like for you.

- Invite friends to share a meal but don't prepare anything different from your normal fare.

- Stop eating out until it becomes a treat once more.

QUESTIONS FOR DISCUSSION AND REFLECTION

1. What sort of recreation re-creates or renews you?

2. Give some examples of drama—a novel, movie, play or song—that have meant a lot to you.

3. Give an example of one of these vacations you might try sometime:

   - a vacation of rest

   - a vacation with a mental purpose

   - a pilgrimage

   - serving others or exploring other cultures

4. What does this chapter lead you to want to pray?

5. Which of the above experiments do you see yourself trying out this week?

9

EVERYDAY LIFE SIMPLICITY

And whatever you do, in word or deed,
do everything in the name of the Lord Jesus,
giving thanks to God the Father through him.

Colossians 3:17

HERE'S SOMETHING TO LOOK FORWARD TO. As your conversations, buying habits and arrangement of time become more focused on treasuring God and loving others, the small tasks of your day will also become more simple. Unburdened by distractions, you'll take on a peaceful, contented, gently examined way of abiding in Christ. Your hurried, autopilot way of doing things will become more straightforward, smooth and integrated. When you find areas that are still complicated and self-indulgent, you'll yearn for simplicity and think of practices that will help you. But in many areas, your tendency toward simplicity will take over. You won't know it until someone mentions it to you.

In this chapter, we'll look at a few areas of everyday life that simplicity might infuse: appearance (clothing, health and fitness), media and technology, but you will no doubt find many more.

Appearance Is All?

Simplicity of appearance flows from the biblical principle of lack of duplicity—not pretending to be someone we're not—and not allowing the outer person to outshine the hidden person of the heart (1 Pet 3:4-5). Peter applied this general principle specifically to women, talking about how elaborate hairstyles and pretentious clothing could overshadow the beauty of the person's spirit, but this fits everyone in our appearance-conscious society.

This transparency of spirit results in an authentic, unaffected way of being. We let nothing distract others from the person we are inside and let nothing deceive others about who we are. This gets at that deep issue of "impression management" discussed in earlier chapters: *Must I manage what others think of me, or can I trust God by being my real self to others?*

> Transparency of spirit results in an authentic, unaffected way of being.

Consider how God might be leading you about how much time, money and energy you put into your appearance. At what point does having an attractive appearance become enslavement for you? Here's a way to begin: take a look at your bathroom. Throw out or give away all but one product for each need—one shampoo, one conditioner, one lotion.

How do you feel when you're doing this? Feelings of panic or scarcity or even confusion can help us discern our true motives: fear, perhaps, of appearing older or plain or unattractive. Beware of our culture's love affair with looking as young as possible, as evidenced by the billion-dollar anti-aging market—it's the fastest growing market in the United States. The current worship of youthfulness causes people to forego celebrating the wisdom and understanding that come with age. Think about what you were like ten years ago: Would you want to be that person again? You might want some of that energy, but the you of today is probably much wiser.

Our purchases always make it obvious when we're serving two masters. A Christian leader confessed to me once that as he looked at his expenditures from the previous year, he saw that every month he spent most of his discretionary money on herbal and cosmetic products that claimed to eliminate wrinkles. What he wanted, it turns out, was to look younger; what he wanted to want was to become wiser and not worry about what impression his appearance made.

Be aware that simplicity of appearance will differ for each of us at different times in our life. For example, after a few years of being consumed with mothering two toddlers, I reexamined what my husband called my "military hairstyle." So mostly for him, I let my cropped hair grow longer and began painting my fingernails. But it was also for me—I needed to remember I was a girl. Then after a while, I seemed to sense God asking me, "Do you really want to devote this much time to fingernails?" Not at all. I had so many other interesting things to do to interact with God and love others.

"Clothes Make the Man"—Really?

This Mark Twain quotation is repeated not only on "dress for success" websites but also in our minds whenever we see someone dressed so that we know she or he put a lot of time and energy into every detail of that one look. Maybe that's appropriate and fun for one's wedding, but that isn't how we are called to live life. Does it represent what you want or the kind of person you want to be?

Simplicity of dress invites us to choose clothes for their usefulness, versatility and ease of movement rather than their ability to make us look drop-dead attractive. The truth is, however, that motives such as pride often lead us to avoid repeating an outfit at work week to week or play one-upmanship in elegant attire at social gatherings. Neediness of soul draws us to engage in retail therapy: "I'm sad, so I'll go buy myself a new ____." Please don't think these temptations apply only to women. Several male students I know have confessed to owning drawers full of workout clothes.

As you become more interested in treasuring God, investing your life in what God is doing and devoting yourself to the good of other people, you'll probably become increasingly indifferent to what you wear. After practicing frugality in many areas, Sharon reports: "I used to spend a lot of time on how I looked compared to others, but not now. My closet is pretty empty. It is easier to decide what to wear this way! Because I am less distracted and concerned about how I appear, I'm more aware of others I meet." Simplicity of appearance simplifies our time and makes it easier to focus on and love other people.

Consider what it means for clothing not to distract from your transparency of spirit. If people see your clothes before they see you (meaning that your clothes stand out to them), there might be something amiss. Provocative clothing can do this; excessively stylish as well as extremely out-of-date clothing can also do this. My rule for what I wear as a speaker or teacher is: Do not distract. I used to wear a vest I enjoyed for its color and classy look. It had different buttons all the way down. After someone told me she was mesmerized by those buttons as I spoke, I never wore it again. To keep packing time to a minimum, I usually wear the same clothes every time I speak, varying only for the sake of formality and informality. People have sometimes commented that I'm wearing the same clothes I was the last time I came to speak. I assure them,

"Don't worry. I've washed them since then."

In the beginning, simplifying clothing may mean choosing a style and colors that look good on you and sticking with these so that you don't need as many. As you progress, consider John Wesley's habit: "As for apparel, I buy the most lasting and, in general, the plainest I can." This sounds strange to most people, but those who dress simply and plainly know that God is the press agent in charge of their reputation. They trust God with other people's opinions of them. Usually they have so many other interesting things in life that they're not bothered by their plainness.

> "As for apparel, I buy the most lasting and, in general, the plainest I can."
>
> *John Wesley*

Simplicity of clothing doesn't mean we can't dress up for celebrations. Nothing about simplicity needs to diminish celebration: in fact, it enhances it because celebrations stand out and become memorable in a life of simplicity.

Health, Fitness and the Glory of God

When talking about the body, Scripture—most notably Proverbs—speaks mostly about excesses such as too much sleep, too much wine or too much food (Prov 6:9; 10:5; 20:1, 13; 23:30-31). Proverbs' other contribution to caring for the body is to talk about how our inner person affects our body. Wholeness and wellness come from exchanging pleasant words, having a tranquil mind, trusting God and turning away from evil, especially runaway emotions that rot the bones (Prov 16:24; 18:8; 3:7-8; 14:30). The Proverbs approach to the body is not to indulge in excess and to keep a right heart.

The apostle Paul offers us the remarkable notion that our bodies can become, as Dallas Willard paraphrases, a "showplace of God's greatness" and even "weapons of righteousness"

(1 Cor 6:20; Rom 8:13). Our bodies can honor God as a worship space for the Holy Spirit (1 Cor 6:19). Especially by means of spiritual disciplines, our lips can be retrained to speak truthfully, lovingly and simply, our arms and legs can be trained to do selfless service and our stomachs and our appetites can know how to both fast and feast. These disciplines position our body as serving our soul, which serves our mind, which serves our will, which serves God.

Our culture, however, suggests that the body dictate to our soul, mind, will and even to God. Whatever it wants it gets and so we serve many cultural masters: indulging our eating a little every day because it doesn't seem like a big deal; making sure to have a body that collects the admiring glances of coworkers; becoming so preoccupied with our health that we take truckloads of vitamins, supplements and rare microorganisms found at the bottom of the ocean. All of these have payoffs: satisfying the appetite, being sexually desirable, being able to do trapeze work at the age of a hundred and ten.

These masters are subtle, especially self-indulgence, which creates in us a soul-corrupting pattern of insisting on getting what we want. This is especially applicable to food. Gluttony, according to C. S. Lewis's Screwtape, is as much about indulging the appetite as excess eating: "A cup of tea properly made, or an egg properly boiled, or a slice of bread properly toasted" can be just as enslaving as a binge eating episode. It's about having one's thoughts wrapped around food and being addicted to the next taste sensation. The addiction is masked because "the quantities involved are small." There's a "determination to get what [we] want, however troublesome it may be." Next time you find yourself on the quest for the perfect sandwich or new taste to tantalize your taste buds, consider how it feels not to have it. What were you hoping it would do for you?

One way we keep the body ready to serve and undistracted is to aim for simplicity, not preoccupation with health issues, scrumptious food or fitness and attractiveness. Simplicity invites us to use sensible self-care, which avoids all those masters and applies the idea of stewardship of the earth (Gen 1:26-30) to responsibly taking care of our body as a blessing from God.

To relinquish preoccupation also means that we control what we can control and surrender the rest. We can manage whether or not we eat proper amounts of food, but we can't control whether the results make us look like Ken or Barbie. We can make sure we get adequate physical exercise, but that may or may not require a gym membership.

When our body is not our master, it can be an arena for the Holy Spirit to work. We can get up in the middle of the night to help someone. We can go without tasty food or a shower on a mission trip. We can climb into a cramped seat on a plane to visit someone who needs us. When the body is uncorrupted by desires to impress or indulge, we can focus squarely on the person standing in front of us or the task we need to complete to be faithful to our work. We become walking temples of the Holy Spirit where there is space to worship God free of distractions.

Information and Media with a Purpose

The many kinds of media now available to us can either help or distract us from intentionally treasuring God and others, depending on how we use them. We can use them to become aware of the needs of the world that God loves and build kinship with others, or we can eat up enormous amounts of time with "idle chatter" (Prov 14:23 NKJV).

To simplify things, ask yourself what you want from media. What kind of person do you want media to help you become? If you want to be informed, what sort of information will build

you into someone who follows hard after God? If that involves
exploring God's creation, magazines such as *Science, Outside* or
National Geographic may help you. When you choose books to
read, think with intentionality
about what God is leading you to
explore next.

What kind of person do
you want media to help
you become?

If your goal is to become aware of
news in the world, you might pick
one or two sources you actually absorb and intentionally limit
your time to those media. Or switch around and use only one
at a time. (Consider also that missionaries as in-the-field repre-
sentatives sometimes provide the best news source.) Think
about if hearing news always slanted to one political view helps
you become a clear thinker. Are you willing to hear the other
side with an open mind and process the pros and cons? Even if
we don't agree, hearing someone else's side often helps us embrace someone we might otherwise regard as an "enemy"—or
at least wrong.

One of my goals in reading news is to know about others'
struggles and desires in life so I may pray for the world God so
loves. I also want to be a clear thinker, so I purposely read opposite views from my own and try to evaluate them without
prejudice. I try to reflect how what I read does or doesn't connect with God's movement throughout history to bring about a
people who become his beloved. This has nudged me to explore
how other cultures think and also how to respect people I dis-
agree with.

Our model in this is Abraham Lincoln, who fought for justice "with malice toward none, with charity for all," even toward political opponents. When Frederick Douglass told Lincoln his second inaugural speech (from which that quote is
taken) was a "sacred effort," he spoke as much about the man

as the speech. Any news outlet we choose needs to help us think deeply, advocate appropriate compassion and move toward justice "with malice toward none, with charity for all."

Consider the role of gossip in media. Gossip doesn't have to be untrue; it can be something that's simply none of my business. Gossip causes us to become distracted from what's important, turning us into "busybodies, saying what [we] should not say" (1 Tim 5:13). If I hear about a famous person's divorce, it's relevant to my life with God only if I know or want to pray for this person. Otherwise it's none of my business. He or she didn't tell me about it. Someone else did. And I was not told with heartbreak or woundedness to arouse appropriate compassion in me.

Such contextless reportage of events teaches me to be callous about other people's calamities. And it tempts me to judge. I think I know this person because I saw her or him play a certain role in a movie, but I don't know this person at all. Sometimes we think we know people because we've seen them on a talk show. Think about how difficult it would be for you to be your real self on a talk show. You probably didn't see that person's real self.

While I don't read magazines about celebrities, I was recently drawn to a newspaper article about two women running for high office and how they seemed to get along now even though they used to be rivals. I got distracted and walked away, which was good, because in the meantime I realized this was gossip. There might be something in the article to reveal these women's character, which is important to me as a voter, but I just wanted the inside scoop. Their squabble and supposed reconciliation were none of my business.

Technology and How It Shapes Us

Pretend for a moment that you're going to fast from email or social networking for two days. How do you feel? Do you fear that you'll be missing out or that you'll be bored? Many people have temporarily simplified their life this way to detox from sensory overload. In chapter three I mentioned the Los Angeles teacher who instituted a seven-day media fast. One of her students reported, "It's an addiction. You don't have to use it, but you get that temptation and it controls you." With students no longer under the spell of the pulsing blue haze of the television or the constant demand of cell phones, the teacher found that their quality of homework vastly improved. The voice on the television, the voice on the cell phone and the person at the other end of the text message no longer called them away from what they intended to do.

God advises us to be careful thinkers who are attentive to wisdom and incline ourselves to understanding (Prov 2:2; 5:1). Followers of Christ need to be clear, careful and intentional thinkers in order to better relate to God, invest in what he is doing and devote ourselves to the good of others. Many studies are now being conducted on how use of the Internet affects our thinking skills. Research so far is inconclusive. But as you use the Internet and hear about these studies, ask yourself some penetrating questions.

- Does my Internet use fill my mind with thoughts that help me love God and love others? Or am I using it for continual self-promotion and idle chatter?

- Does my Internet use help me think well? How does it affect my reading ability? Can I still read books with depth? How is it affecting my need to reflect?

- Does my Internet use promote shallowness of thinking in any way so that I mistake surface-level familiarity with deep understanding? Is it convincing me that because I have access to so many facts and figures that I'm smarter or wiser than I am?

These questions bring us back to the heart exam: *What do I want? What do I really want? What do I long for?* We need to examine our Internet use in light of how it can—or can't—help me become the person I really want to be.

Imparting Grace in Email

With email reinventing letter writing, it requires us to apply sensible judgment. "You'll say things over the Internet that you would not [say] in person or in a letter," says John Freeman, who receives two hundred to three hundred messages a day as president of the National Book Critics Circle. With email, "you don't have any of the usual visual cues from face-to-face communication or in a conversation over the phone. There are no pauses, no pregnant silences—you can't see someone wince when you say something rude. Or they might see you going in a direction and start to show visible anxiety. Writing over email, you have none of that."

Freeman also hazards this guess: "Psychologically, there's something that happens when you spend more time with a computer than you do with your spouse. Staring at it all day. It becomes a kind of extension of your mind. . . . The more we withdraw from the real world, the less we're invested in it."

As an introverted, task-oriented person, I confess I love email because I love getting a job done without having to actually talk to anyone, but I also know that God is teaching me to be more relational and that using email can work for or against that, depending on how I use it. So my goal is to use it as I use speech: to impart grace to others (Eph 4:29). Sometimes I need to place my reply to an email in the drafts folder and leave it there for an hour or a day or a week. Now and then I ask my husband to read a message before I send it out. Based on how his eyes sometimes bulge, I still have a lot to learn about imparting grace.

A few years ago, I began noticing that I was trying to clear out my inbox at lightning speed. Imparting grace to others wasn't at the front of my mind. So I began intentionally approaching a full inbox without dread (well, this is my intention anyway—and most days it happens!) and trying to think of the best way to address each person.

My newer approach is not as efficient time-wise, which means it has been one more moment in my life where I've decided that having my editors praise me for "always being on top of things" is not my goal. Instead this approach aligns with my decision many years ago to live intentionally by asking these two questions: *What would it look like to love God for the next ten minutes? What would it look like to love others in the next ten minutes?* This less efficient but more intentional way of answering email has come about because of those two questions.

Regarding the ubiquitous cell phone, the current theory seems to be: I must have the latest technology, and I must utilize it at all times. But to know what we want most helps us make decisions about cell phones. If our goal is to have direct, unpretentious, unencumbered relationships with others and to show courtesy to strangers, we need to intentionally be wise and kind in our cell phone use. Unlimited clutching of one's cell phone may get in the way of loving people. It can change the sort of attention we give them and cause us to be impolite. That's not who I intend to be.

Disciplines of simplicity invite us to interrupt the norm and go without, so you might want to turn your cell phone off for a day (or an hour) and see how that feels. This makes the heart exam of simplicity up-close and personal: What does it tell us that we believe we must be always available to the world? How does it affect our understanding of Sabbath?

I'm fascinated by how often my students choose to fast from technology—cell phones or Facebook or even computer use—when we study fasting and they are required to do an experiment. One student who fasted from cell phone use reported, "With the cell phone turned off, I realized that I'm not as important as I make myself out to be. The world goes on even when I'm not connected to it." This is significant formational work. It can help us curb whatever enslavement, self-indulgence and impression management tendencies are at work in us and treasure both God's own self and those around us.

The Saturation Factor

The ripple effect of simplicity causes it to spill over to relationships. Author Peter Walsh observes that after people organize and declutter their homes, "almost without exception, people reassess their relationships and remove the hurdles that have stunted their emotional lives. . . . People have lost weight, changed careers, reassessed the way they spend their time, altered the way they interact with their friends and family, and reorganized their priorities." With simpler speech, we no longer feel forced to say conventional words we don't mean. We're free to like people more because we didn't have to buy something new or clean our house from top to bottom to impress them.

That's why simplicity of life often eases resentment that has played itself out in selfishness or withdrawal. As we become intentional about giving people time, listening to them (without answering a ringing cell phone) and making eye contact, our own heart is changed and these resentments drop off. We live more authentically in our relationships, whether that's with a best friend or the customer service representative at the auto parts store.

You might ask God what other areas you could explore for greater simplicity: your work life, what your yard looks like, your participation in church, your approach to worship or the music you listen to. In every area we ask: *What do I want? What am I longing for? What am I being invited to do to treasure God and love others?*

EXPERIMENTS WITH ORDINARY, EVERYDAY TASKS

- Look at your personal health and beauty products and determine which ones are about sensible self-care and which ones are about something else, such as trying to look younger.

- Pick out some plain clothes to wear for one day. How does it feel to consider wearing this simple outfit? (Even if you don't wear it, this is a good exercise.) If you're able, wear this plain clothing for a day. Journal about how you felt when you walked into a room. How many days in a row could you dress simply and plainly?

- Pick out a piece of clothing or two that does not in any way deceive anyone about what you're like. Why is that so?

- Write down or talk with someone about your health and fitness goals. What do you really want?

- Exercise sensibly and regularly for a week in gratefulness that God gave you a body that is the finest invention in the world.

- Ask God about your sources of news, being open to whatever you need to know.

- Log your Internet use for a day or two. Then evaluate: How did it help you love God and others? How did it help you set your thoughts on God or become a more careful thinker?

- Try an email or cell phone fast for a certain length of time. Journal or talk to someone about the feelings that arise within you.

QUESTIONS FOR DISCUSSION
AND REFLECTION

1. What sort of simplicity of appearance would you like to try out?

2. Put into words an approach to fitness that you think honors God and aims for simplicity.

3. What sources of news or information help you glorify God in some way?

4. What does this chapter lead you to want to pray?

5. Which of the above experiments do you see yourself trying out this week?

10

WORRY NO LONGER NECESSARY

Therefore do not worry, saying, "What will we eat?"
or "What will we drink?" or "What will we wear?"
For it is the Gentiles who strive for all these things;
and indeed your heavenly Father knows that you need all these things.
But strive first for the kingdom of God and his righteousness,
and all these things will be given to you as well.
So do not worry about tomorrow, for tomorrow will bring worries of its own.
Today's trouble is enough for today.

Matthew 6:31-34

WHEN I FIRST BEGAN TRAVELING AND SPEAKING, it seemed necessary to worry about what I'd eat, drink and wear (Mt 6:25, 31). Would I find anything nourishing in airports that would give me long-lasting energy? Could I look presentable with all the havoc that travel and packing wreak on clothes? Would this plane get me to the event on time?

Simplicity saved me. I routinely took protein powder to shake in orange juice for meals, wore the same sweats to fly in and the same clothes to speak in and left margins of time between flights instead of playing it close. While at times I still have to breathe the twenty-third psalm while running through an airport, worry no longer seems obligatory. A growing faith helps, but embracing simplicity makes it easier to have that faith.

In this book we've focused on trusting God and interacting with him. Simplicity is merely the "delivery system"—a way to connect with God. Because of this emphasis on knowing God, we've looked at parts of Jesus' Sermon on the Mount (Mt 6:19-34). In the first three chapters we talked about how practices of simplicity help us live out the reality that God's own self is our treasure in heaven. This treasure is available to us now, and we can draw on God for today's needs (Mt 6:19-21). With God as our treasure, we live with more intentionality, keeping our eye "single" (Mt 6:22-23 KJV). Such intentionality helps us give up on the impossible, crazy-making dynamic of trying to serve two masters: God and self-promotion, God and money, God and looking good (Mt 6:24).

Such simplicity of life, says Jesus, means that we "therefore" need no longer worry:

> Therefore I tell you, do not worry about your life, what you will eat or what you will drink, or about your body, what you will wear. Is not life more than food, and the body more than clothing? Look at the birds of the air; they neither sow nor reap nor gather into barns, and yet your heavenly Father feeds them. Are you not of more value than they? And can any of you by worrying add a single hour to your span of life? And why do you worry about clothing? Consider the lilies of the field, how they grow; they neither toil nor spin, yet I tell you, even Solomon in all his glory was not clothed like one of these. But if God so clothes the grass of the field, which is alive today and

tomorrow is thrown into the oven, will he not much more clothe you—you of little faith? (Mt 6:25-30)

Worry is not necessary when we seek God, God's kingdom and God's deep inner goodness, because then "all these things will be given" to us (Mt 6:33). "All these things" includes not only what we'll eat, drink and wear but also wisdom, safety and fulfillment as well as whatever reputation, achievements, affluence and appearance God thinks we need.

Yet we're reluctant to let go of our worry. We worry about not worrying. Many of us even believe that worrying about something earns us the right for nothing bad to happen. It's as if the more minutes of worry time we accrue, the less likely we are to experience problems. Jesus sensed our reluctance to stop worrying, so he presented the absurd proposition that worrying could actually earn us an additional full hour in our life span (Mt 6:27).

Such distortions are the enemy's work, convincing us that worry is a form of responsible vigilance. I might reason, for example, that if I dwell on the likelihood of my wallet being stolen while traveling, the theft won't occur. It's as if we're unconsciously making a deal with God: If I suffer enough by worrying, you won't make me suffer more by learning a lesson through adversity.

Perhaps also to help us let go of worry, Jesus woos us into a vision of a worry-free life with funny word pictures. Imagine a tiny sparrow pushing a huge iron or wooden plow hard enough to create a deep furrow in Middle Eastern soil. Or imagine a whole flock of birds reaping a crop and whisking it into barn after barn. (This has no doubt happened in a Walt Disney movie or two, but Jesus' listeners hadn't seen any of them.) In God's

We worry about not worrying.

typically generous, self-giving way of grace, he does not require birds to do the hard work of many field hands but instead provides his creatures with what they need.

Or imagine a giant field lily sitting before a spinning wheel with its petals carefully positioning fibers so they can be spun into thread or yarn. (Would it have to keep its blooms out of the way?) Or picture that same field lily standing at a large loom, guiding the threads along. Jesus exclaims over these tiny flowers, asking his listeners to just look at how they grow! (Can you see him staring at the ground in wonder, arms wide open?)

Out of uncultivated, overlooked soil comes something more beautiful than the best fashions Paris can offer. Or, if he were speaking today, Jesus might say the field lily was more beautiful than an Italian sports car or a spectacular play in sports. Jesus seems to be telling us not only that worry is illogical and bizarre but also that God's care of us is so detailed and exquisite that we can stand amazed at it, if we pay attention (Mt 6:28-29).

As his listeners undoubtedly chuckled at his pictures, Jesus invited them in his not-so-upscale Galilean accent to consider life with God beginning now. It might have sounded to his hearers' ears something like this:

> So cut out your anxious talk about "what are we gonna eat, and what are we gonna drink, and what are we gonna wear." For the people of the world go tearing around after all these things. Listen, your spiritual Father is quite aware that you've got to have all such stuff. Then set your heart on the God Movement and its kind of life, and all these things will come as a matter of course.

Jesus seemed to know that seeking simplicity—particularly in regard to food, clothing and appearance—is a journey. He comforts us by saying that God knows we need all these things and that they will be given to us as we seek God and the kingdom. Jesus wasn't saying these things don't matter. The tunic he himself wore was so special that his executioners didn't tear it up but threw dice for it. Because these things matter, we can trust God to provide them for us.

Much More God

While I was meditating on Matthew 6:19-34, the phrase "much more" in verse 30—"will he not much more clothe you"—stood before me and sparkled. Where I grew up there was a hilly, zigzagging road called Muchmore Road. It deserved that name, because when people drove it they wondered, *How much more of this can I stand?* But my mother liked to drive that road. Since it was an alternate route out of town, she would ask me when we got near the cutoff, "Do you want to take Muchmore Road?"

She said it with a gleam in her eye that told me we were in for great fun. I always said, "Yes, let's take Muchmore!" Unlike other drivers, my mother was sorry when she got to the end. She was never too tired to drive it. When I learned to drive, I always took Muchmore as well. So when I picture Jesus saying, "Will he not much more clothe you?" I guess I see my mother's gleam in his eye as he says it.

That phrase "much more" occurs many times in Scripture and usually indicates God's astonishing generosity (see Mt 7:11; Rom 5:9-10, 15, 17; 2 Cor 3:7-11). If, however, we believe that God is forcing us to live a "much less" life, practices of simplicity will seem scary. It will seem necessary to worry, especially that simplicity practices will deprive us in some way.

So our view of God is important. If we think God rewards us with no suffering when we worry about suffering, we have a "much less" God. Speaking about this passage in Matthew, scholar Tom Wright says:

> When [Jesus] urged them to make God their priority, it's important to realize which God he's talking about. He's not talking about a god who is distant from the world, who doesn't care about beauty and life and food and clothes. He's talking about the creator himself, who has filled the world with wonderful and mysterious things, full of beauty and energy and excitement and who wants his human creatures above all to trust him and love him and receive their own beauty, energy and excitement from him.

Jesus knew God to be a God of much more, so it was natural for him to say, "Give your entire attention to what God is doing right now, and don't get worked up about what may or may not happen tomorrow. God will help you deal with whatever hard things come up when the time comes" (Mt 6:34 *The Message*).

Jesus knew God to be a God of much more.

Jesus shows us that we don't need to worry when our treasure (God) is in heaven, our eye is single-focused and healthy, and we're not struggling to serve two masters. Simplicity helps us be present and attentive to the task at hand, enjoying God's goodness here and now. We can approach each event of our upcoming day by asking God: How might I, with your miraculous power, love you and serve you when:

- my colleague comes to help me adjust my computer?
- I work out?
- I welcome a friend I'm meeting with?
- I practice Sabbath for a few minutes?
- you allow adventurous interruptions?

We now recognize the thieves that break in and steal our treasure. They're the attention we give to making sure we're loved and valued by the right people, to trying to appear better than we really are, and to projecting what we might miss out on if we don't do certain things. Simplicity practices redirect that attention to trust in God.

Don't Worry About Simplicity Either

Worry is clutter of the mind that doesn't go away. If we're not experiencing the life God promised, it is often because we have cluttered our minds with confusing thoughts and worries. And now we might also worry about how we'll practice simplicity: *Am I doing this right? Should I be doing more? What if I don't want to do this? What if my cell phone is my best friend? What if I'm hooked on thinking about what others think of me?*

Keep in mind that disciplines of simplicity are about life with God, not about whether we're doing a certain discipline right. Here are some ideas that might help you approach them with God's generous, self-giving way of grace.

We start with ourselves. We need to give up the idea that our way is also the way others should practice simplicity. Setting ourselves up as the standard is arrogant, of course, but it's also impractical. We're all in different places in our walk with God and live in different circumstances.

Richard Foster confesses, "There once was a time when I urged simplicity of life upon people indiscriminately. I would cajole, shove, push, and often they would indeed change their lifestyle, but I found that it was all quite destructive. I discovered that simplicity is just another anxiety-laden burden until people have experienced God's gracious power to provide them with daily bread. Only as Kingdom power breaks in are we free to live in trust." Disciplines are only a means to life with God

ABUNDANT SIMPLICITY

158

and will not matter unless we understand a little of what that
life looks like and desire it.

We cannot assume that every member of our household will
be in favor of everything we want to do. As you make small
decisions, inform those you live with if they're affected, but
otherwise don't make an announcement. Work it out for yourself. As you do so, others will probably notice and may or may
not decide to join you. That is the other person's choice.

For example, if you choose to stop watching TV, just do it.
Spend your time as you wish. Drop by the group watching TV
to wave or give a hug from behind, but then keep going. Your
goal is not to snub anyone but to figure out what you really
want in your life and make space for it. You may be surprised
that others join you now and then—you may even decide to
make the change permanent.

If you'd like someone to experiment with you, you might ask
several people to join you. Even in those cases, exchange ideas
but don't talk about it a lot. Lengthy discussions about simplicity usually sabotage it, often by creating pride about how simply wonderful we are. Much of what we can do to simplify can
happen without anyone else's involvement: how we speak, how
we dress, how many kinds of shampoo we own.

Any amount of time counts. We don't have to do a certain
practice for a lifetime. We can limit shopping during Lent; we
can give our lunch money away just today; we can try out a new
service commitment that seems to fit our calling on a tempo-
rary basis only. It's important to reflect on these things in the
heart exam posture. Maybe you learned from the practice but
you won't be able to do it continually. That's fine. Some practices, such as fasting, are most effective when we do them now
and then.

We don't compare ourselves with others. What speaks of simplicity to one person does not always resonate with another. Planting a garden is simple and fun for some, but for others it's a complicated chore. Wearing three basic colors is a welcome relief to some but a creativity stifler for others.

My husband and I have friends who own only one car. They can easily afford two, but they've chosen to spend their money this way so they have more to give. For a while I felt guilty whenever we were around them. Then I realized they weren't thinking about our two cars at all. So I felt freer to say to God, "If you think having one car is a good idea, I need to say I'm not ready for that, OK? If you want me to be ready for that, please get me there." Thankfully, God has not shown me that. The goal is to listen to God, not to impress others or ourselves.

We do things as we are ready. A simplicity practice should challenge us somewhat but not too much. We don't force ourselves into things we really don't want to do. When William Penn asked George Fox if it was right for him to continue wearing his sword (since Quakers favored "gentler forces of the Spirit"), Fox told him, "'Wear it as long as thou canst'; *i.e.,* wear it until conscience makes it clear that a sword is not consistent with Christian life and profession." Fox laid down no rules and invited people to look to inward guidance.

So we don't try to be heroic. I stopped watching TV when I could no longer stand to hand over so much of my life to it. I wanted those hours for other things. I don't ever miss not watching TV. Also, what works best for you will change because you are continually changing. Nothing replaces continual conversation with God. Nothing.

We don't take our spirituality too seriously. All these heart exams are going to reveal self-absorption and overconcern with the three A's: achievement, affluence and appearance. We have to get over ourselves, as I said in the beginning, and not let our tendency toward self distract us. The Spirit is the one who does the reforming; we candidly admit our mistakes and ask for a simple next step. We don't become discouraged that we are not perfect. My spirituality is not about me but about God.

We focus on the next step. You may experiment with many practices later on, but the most important question is, *What is God leading me to do today?* Try one of the experiments for only a day and either journal about it or talk about it with a friend. In a week or a month, come back to this book and reread what you may have underlined

> My spirituality is not about me but about God.

or highlighted or especially noted. Then ask God again, *What is my next step?* Our next steps may seem pathetically small but that's OK. It's not about accomplishing big things but about walking with Jesus.

We make room for celebration and beauty. Simplicity is not necessarily austerity. Jesus enjoyed festivals and celebrations and made sure a certain wedding didn't run out of wine. In Dorothy Day's houses of hospitality in the slums of New York, the surroundings were meager but she liked for them to be bright, sunny and attractive with pictures on the walls. She was profoundly attentive to beauty and managed to find it in places where it was often overlooked—in nature, in a piece of bread, in the smell of garlic drifting out a tenement window, or in flowers blooming in a slum neighborhood.

Practices of simplicity are positive as well as negative. They end up creating a life of much by choosing a life of less. They help us turn toward the face of our "much more God" for interaction and conversation. It really can happen now that our life has space for that kind of dynamic relationship to occur.

EXPERIMENTS WITH SIMPLICITY

- Write down your next steps. Look at the list. Talk to God about anything about these steps that mildly terrifies you or creates pride at how supposedly advanced you will seem if you do them. (If you wish, you can also make this list: "Possible next steps after that.")

- Go back through this book and look at what you have underlined. Then set the book down. What do you now want to pray? Are there any ideas or phrases from the book that might help you in your prayers?

- If you feel impatient to grow, savor the first line of Pierre Teilhard de Chardin's poem prayer "Patient Trust": "Above all, trust in the slow work of God."

- Study Matthew 6:19-34. Think about the ideas of treasuring God, single-focused intentionality and not serving two masters. How might those things lead you not to worry and to seek God above all else?

- Meditate on Matthew 6:25-30 and try to imagine Jesus' pictures of birds pushing plows and lilies weaving. If you wish, make a sketch of them.

QUESTIONS FOR DISCUSSION AND REFLECTION

1. Has your view of God been a "much more" view or a "much less" one?

2. What circumstance or activities in your life would you like to put in this blank? How might I treasure God when I _____?

3. Which of the ideas about approaching simplicity disciplines with grace are the most helpful to you?

4. What does this chapter lead you to want to pray?

5. Which of the above experiments do you see yourself trying out this week?

ACKNOWLEDGMENTS

I OWE A DELIGHTFUL DEBT TO FRIENDS, students and "wisbit" list recipients (www.JanJohnson.org/wisbits.html) who emailed me stories about simplicity. These include Tabitha Dileo, Larae Doose, Janice Hill, Cathleen Jackson, Lisa Lewis, Sandra Linderman, Fred Napier, Sharon Rowland, Carol Summerell and Peggy Walcott. I also owe special thanks to Teine Kenney of Organize This (www.organizethishome.com) for her emails and telephone interview.

Thanks is also due the Simi Valley Public Library librarians who fulfill my many interlibrary loan requests and now stack them for me when they see me walk through the doors into the library.

As always, editors provide a second voice and Cindy Bunch has nudged out of me much more than I expected. I'm always grateful to my husband, Greg, who goes over all my books (this one twice!), and adult children, Janae and Jeff. All three seem to have been born knowing more about simplicity than Mom did.

NOTES

Chapter 1: Abundant Life with God

page 8   It is an "inward reality": *Renovaré Spiritual Formation Bible* (San Francisco: HarperSanFrancisco, 2005), p. 2313.

page 10   "The most important commandment": Dallas Willard, *The Divine Conspiracy: Rediscovering Our Hidden Life in God* (San Francisco: HarperSanFrancisco, 1998), p. 203.

page 10   investing our life: Ibid., p. 205.

page 12   "Nothing is more practical": Fr. Pedro Arrupe, quoted in Richard Rohr, *Everything Belongs: The Gift of Contemplative Prayer* (New York: Crossroad, 2003), p. 122.

page 17   twin themes: Thomas á Kempis *Imitation of Christ* 1.3.4.

page 17   "getting up, dressing": Tom Morris, *Philosophy for Dummies* (New York: Wiley, 1999), p. 17.

page 20   prayer of *examen*: An excellent but simple resource for the prayer of *examen* is Dennis Linn, Sheila Fabricant Linn and Matthew Linn, *Sleeping with Bread* (Mahwah, N.J.: Paulist, 1995).

page 20   "Above all, trust": Pierre Teilhard de Chardin, "Patient Trust," in *Hearts on Fire: Praying with Jesuits*, ed. Michael Harter, S.J. (St. Louis: Institute of Jesuit Sources, 1993), p. 58.

Chapter 2: Coping with Plenty

page 24   One person interviewed: Associated Press, "Religion Isn't Curbing Materialism, Poll Says," *Los Angeles Times*, September 24, 1994, pp. B10-B11. See also Robert Wuthnow, *God and Mammon in America* (New York: Free Press, 1998).

page 24   "We live in a materialistic": Ibid.

page 26   7-Eleven tested: Patrick Kiger, "Living Ever Larger," *Los Ange-les Times Magazine,* June 9, 2002, p. 12.

page 26   "the pursuit of self-interest": Richard Foster, *The Freedom of Simplicity* (San Francisco: Harper & Row, 1981), p. 175.

page 29   deny ourselves a little: William James, *Psychology: Briefer Course,* in *Writings 1878-1899* (New York: Library of America, 1992), p. 150.

page 31   "Marketing theory says": Vicki Robin and Joe Dominguez, *Your Money or Your Life* (New York: Penguin, 2002), p. 18.

page 32   These wounds: Many excellent books exist to help us face fears and work through them. If you need to get started, see this free online book: Jan Johnson, *Healing Hurts That Sabotage the Soul* (1995), <www.janjohnson.org/healing_hurts_that_sabotage_th.html>.

page 32   "interior castle": Teresa of Avila, *The Interior Castle,* trans. Kieran Kavanaugh and Otioio Rodriguez, The Classics of Western Spirituality (Mahwah, N.J.: Paulist, 1979).

page 33   spiritual exercises of Ignatius: These questions are discussed by many sources, including John O'Keefe, "What Do You Want?" (October 7, 2009), This Ignatian Life <ignatianlife.org/what-do-you-want/>.

page 33   In trying to discern: Bruce Wydick, "Where Your Treasure Is," *Prism,* March-April 2009, p. 21.

page 33   "I can tell": Ibid.

page 34   "will keep [us]": Dallas Willard, *Renovation of the Heart* (Colorado Springs: NavPress, 2002), p. 9.

page 35   Our admiration for Jesus: Dallas Willard, "Spirituality and Ministry" (lecture given at Fuller Seminary, June 19, 2002, class notes by Jan Johnson).

page 36   "Disregarding all those things": Gregory of Nyssa, *The Life of Moses,* trans. Abraham Malherbe and Everett Ferguson, The Classics of Western Spirituality (Mahwah, N.J.: Paulist, 1978), p. 137.

Chapter 3: What Do You Really Want?

page 39   "if therefore thine eye": Newer versions have chosen medical terms such as "healthy" or "good" instead of "single," but the

King James Version's terminology works well with verse 33: "Seek ye first . . ."

page 41   "decide everything": Fr. Pedro Arrupe, quoted in Richard Rohr, *Everything Belongs: The Gift of Contemplative Prayer* (New York: Crossroad, 2003), p. 122.

page 43   craving for variety: Søren Kierkegaard, "Purity of Heart: Edifying Discourses in Various Spirits," in *A Kierkegaard Anthology*, ed. Robert Bretall, trans. Douglas Steere (New York: Modern Library, 1946), pp. 271-74.

page 44   he began as a vain young man: John Woolman, *The Journal of John Woolman* (New York: Corinth Books, 1961), pp. vii-x, 5-21.

page 45   One evening after preaching: This story is told in Richard Foster, *Streams of Living Water* (San Francisco: HarperSanFrancisco, 1998), p. 139.

page 45   he already sensed: Woolman, *Journal*, pp. vii-x, 5-21.

page 46   "In every action": Jeremy Taylor, *Selected Works*, The Classics of Western Spirituality (Mahwah, N.J.: Paulist, 1990), p. 444.

page 47   "I wished to live deliberately": Henry David Thoreau, *Walden* (New York: Dodd, Mead, 1946), p. 72.

page 47   "If you and I": Evelyn Underhill, *The Ways of the Spirit*, ed. Grace Adolphsen Brame (New York: Crossroad, 1990), p. 160.

page 49   "When people control": Paula Huston, *The Holy Way: Practices for a Simple Life* (Chicago: Loyola Press, 2003), p. xiv.

page 50   In a Los Angeles college-prep: Steve Lopez, "The Rigors of Life Unplugged," *Los Angeles Times*, May 6, 2009, p. A2.

page 51   "Simplicity is freedom": Richard Foster, *Celebration of Discipline* (San Francisco: Harper & Row, 1988), p. 79.

Interlude: What Simplicity Might Look Like
page 55   "Pray as you can": John Chapman, *Spiritual Letters* (London: Sheed & Ward, 1935), p. 25.

Chapter 4: Fewness and Fullness of Words
page 57   Quaker founder George Fox: *Quaker Spirituality: Selected Writings*, ed. Douglas Steere. The Classics of Western Spirituality (Mahwah, N.J.: Paulist, 1984), p. 61.

page 57   William Penn went on: Ibid.

page 60   As long as they didn't swear: William Barclay, *The Gospel of Matthew*, The Daily Study Bible (Philadelphia: Westminster Press, 1958), p. 157.

page 60   "Faith does not need": Richard Rohr, *Everything Belongs: The Gift of Contemplative Prayer* (New York: Crossroad, 2003), p. 143.

page 61   "the main thoroughfare of evil": Dallas Willard, *The Spirit of the Disciplines* (San Francisco: Harper & Row, 1988), p. 228.

page 61   "Many a time I wish": Thomas à Kempis *The Imitation of Christ* 1.10.

page 62   "Simplicity, meekness and modesty": Francis de Sales, *Introduction to the Devout Life* (New York: Doubleday, 1972), p. 190.

page 64   when Samuel Johnson was asked: James Boswell, *The Life of Samuel Johnson* (New York: Modern Library, 1952), p. 644.

page 65   "Speech becomes truthful": Richard Foster, *Celebration of Discipline* (San Francisco: Harper & Row, 1988), p. 80.

page 67   "It is a wholesome act": Shirley Carter Hughson, *With Christ in God* (New York: Holy Cross, 1947), pp. 196-97.

page 68   "Remember: the most interesting person": Tom Wright, *Paul for Everyone: The Prison Letters* (Louisville, Ky.: Westminster John Knox, 2004), p. 99.

Chapter 5: Living Light in a Land of Plenty

page 75 $7,000 a year: "Average Earnings Worldwide," *The Boston Globe*, October 7, 2007, <www.boston.com/news/world/articles /2007/10/07/average_earnings_worldwide/>.

page 76   "Its Latin root, *frux*": James Nash, "Frugality: Antidote to Prodigality," *Journal of Lutheran Ethics* 7, no. 1 (2007) <www .elca.org/What-We-Believe/Social-Issues/Journal-of-Lutheran-Ethics/Issues/January-2007/Frugality-Antidote-to-Prodigal ity.aspx>.

page 77   increasing income creates: Vicki Robin and Joe Dominguez, *Your Money or Your Life* (New York: Penguin, 2008), pp. 21-25. See also <http://newroadmap.pbworks.com/w/page/10458661/ The-Fulfillment-Curve>.

page 78   despite the fact: Bruce Wydick, "Where Your Treasure Is,"

Prism, March-April 2009, p. 21.

page 78   "Americans have apparently": John Austin, "American's Race for Space Fuels Boom in Self-Storage," *Champaign News-Gazette*, September 17, 2005, p. C-7.

page 78   "'Upward mobility' often ends": Robert C. Roberts, "Just a Little Bit More," *Christianity Today*, April 8, 1996, p. 30.

page 79   "If you were at a store": Teine Kenney, interview by Jan Johnson, April 7, 2009. See also <www.organizethishome.com>.

page 79   "Everything stashed away": Don Aslett, *Is There Life After Housework?* (Cincinnati: Writer's Digest Books, 1981), pp. 24-26, as quoted in Ruth Tucker, *The Christian Speaker's Treasury* (San Francisco: Harper & Row, 1989), p. 189.

page 81   "If you haven't used it": Elaine St. James, *The Simplicity Reader* (New York: Hyperion, 1998), p. 12

page 83   "God, of your goodness": Julian of Norwich, *Showings*, trans. Edmund Colledge and James Walsh, The Classics of Western Spirituality (Mahwah, N.J.: Paulist, 1978), p. 184.

Chapter 6: A Generous, Not Grasping, Life

page 89   "A theology of consumption": Evy McDonald, "Spending Money as if Life Really Mattered," in *Simpler Living, Compassionate Life: A Christian Perspective*, ed. Michael Schut (Denver: Living the Good News, 1999), p. 60.

page 89   outnumber high schools: "Consumption by the United States," Mindfully.org <www.mindfully.org/Sustainability/Americans-Consume-24percent.htm>.

page 90   "The spiritually wise person": Dallas Willard, *The Spirit of the Disciplines* (San Francisco: Harper & Row, 1988), p. 169.

page 90   "Our culture is little inclined": Robert C. Roberts, "Just a Little Bit More," *Christianity Today*, April 8, 1996, p. 30.

page 91   Every budget: Ron Sider, "Evaluating President Bush's 2006 Budget," *Prism*, July-August 2005, p. 40.

page 92   Well-developed countries: "Consumption by the United States," Mindfully.org <www.mindfully.org/Sustainability/Americans-Consume-24percent.htm>.

page 92   "The moral problem is not": James Nash, "Frugality: Antidote to Prodigality," *Journal of Lutheran Ethics* 7, no. 1 (2007) <www

.elca.org/What-We-Believe/Social-Issues/Journal-of-Lutheran-Ethics/Issues/January-2007/Frugality-Antidote-to-Prodigal ity.aspx>.

page 93   "We buy things": Peter Walsh, *Enough Already! Clearing Mental Clutter to Become the Best You* (New York: Free Press, 2009), p. 2.

page 94   "Business has been dominating": "Bill Hybels Talks REVEAL," LeadershipJournal.net, March 6, 2009 <www.christianitytoday .com/le/communitylife/discipleship/billhybelstalksreveal.html>.

page 94   Love of novelty: I got this idea from William Barclay, *The Letters to Timothy, Titus and Philemon*, The Daily Study Bible (Philadelphia: Westminster Press, 1960), p. 207.

page 95   If shopping becomes: For help, consider visiting a Spenders Anonymous meeting <www.spenders.org>. Debtors Anonymous <www.debtorsanonymous.org> offers a mentoring system for budget accountability.

page 97   "The point is not": Richard Foster, *The Freedom of Simplicity* (San Francisco: Harper & Row, 1981), p. 122.

page 97   The thirty-day list: Elaine St. James, *The Simplicity Reader* (New York: Hyperion, 1998), p. 680.

page 98   Consider that the average: Ibid., p. 161.

page 99   God is "generous": Tom Wright, *Luke for Everyone* (Louisville, Ky.: Westminster John Knox, 2004), pp. 73-74.

Chapter 7: The Intentional, Unhurried Life

page 104   "little time for love": Gerald May, *The Awakened Heart* (San Francisco: HarperSanFrancisco, 1991), p. 100.

page 107   "In recovering the Sabbath": Ron Sider, "Consumers, Advertisers, Workaholics and the Sabbath," *Prism*, September-October 1996, p. 42.

page 108   Sabbath was made for us: For more about Sabbath, see this simple but excellent book: Lynne M. Baab, *Sabbath Keeping* (Downers Grove, Ill.: InterVarsity Press, 2005).

page 109   God was bringing to my attention: Richard Swenson, *Margin: Restoring Emotional, Physical, Financial, and Time Reserves to Overloaded Lives* (Colorado Springs: NavPress, 2004).

page 111   "This was extremely uncomfortable": Paula Huston, *The Holy*

Way: Practices for a Simple Life (Chicago: Loyola Press, 2003), pp. 173-74.

page 111   Many books and seminars: I first used material based on Edward R. Dayton and Ted W. Engstrom, *Strategy for Living: How to Make the Best Use of Your Time and Abilities* (Ventura, Calif.: Regal, 1976). For more details on how to use this method, see: "Time Management: Living with Intentionality" at <www.jan johnson.org/articles__spiritual_growth_-_t1.html>.

page 111   Once you have your list: Richard Foster, *The Freedom of Simplicity* (San Francisco: Harper & Row, 1981), p. 92.

page 114   One of the greatest: For a full treatment of this topic, see Jan Johnson, *Living a Purpose-Full Life* (City, Waterbrook, 1999).

page 115   "The Loving Presence": Thomas Kelly, *A Testament of Devotion* (New York: Walker, 1987), pp. 149-50.

page 115   "the place where": Frederick Buechner, *Wishful Thinking: A Theological ABC* (New York: Harper & Row, 1973), p. 95.

Chapter 8: Putting the "Free" in Free Time

page 119   "We worship our work": Gordon Dahl, *Work, Play and Worship in a Leisure-Oriented Society,* (Minneapolis: Augsburg, 1972), p. 12, as quoted in Tim Hansel, *When I Relax I Feel Guilty,* (Elgin, Ill.: David C. Cook, 1979), p. 33.

page 120   thirty-nine percent: "Global Workers Prefer Leisure," *USA Today* (Society for the Advancement of Education), April 1996. <http://findarticles.com/p/articles/mi_m1272/is_n2611_v124/ai_18232459/>.

page 120   "watched the birds": Tom Wright, *Matthew for Everyone, Part 1* (Louisville, Ky.: Westminster John Knox, 2004), p. 65.

page 120   "The leisure activities": C. S. Lewis, "Civilization," *The Quotable Lewis*, ed. Wayne Martindale and Jerry Root (Wheaton, Ill.: Tyndale House, 1989), p. 112.

page 120   "Our leisure, even our play": C. S. Lewis, "Christianity and Literature," *Christian Reflections* (Grand Rapids: Eerdmans, 1967), p. 33.

page 122   "Much recreation does not": Richard Rohr, *Everything Belongs: The Gift of Contemplative Prayer* (New York: Crossroad, 2003), p. 54.

page 124   "A person should hear": Johann von Goethe, quoted in *The Spiritual Formation Bible* (Grand Rapids: Zondervan, 1999), p. 421.

page 125   "Having attached personal memories": Christian George, "The Pilgrim Way: Discovering the Ancient Practice of Pilgrimage," *Conversations* 5, no. 2 (2007): 76

page 125   "No AAA tour book": Dale Painter, "Extra-Value Vacations," *Discipleship Journal* 97 (1997): 32-33.

page 127   "It's good to enrich our life": Dallas Willard, "Spirituality and Ministry" (lecture given at Fuller Seminary, June 11, 2009, class notes by Jan Johnson).

page 127   Jesus provides drama: For more about this, see Jan Johnson, *Invitation to the Jesus Life* (Colorado Springs: NavPress, 2008), pp. 212-19.

page 127   more than four hours: "Television and Health," California State University, Northridge <www.csun.edu/science/health/docs/tv&health.html>.

page 131   One organization: See <www.altgifts.org> and <www.janjohnson.org/articles__compassion_-_alterna.html>.

Chapter 9: Everyday Life Simplicity

page 136   billion-dollar anti-aging market: "Pharmaceuticals: Antiaging Products and Services" (February 2005), BCC Research <www.bccresearch.com/report/PHM041A.html>.

page 139   "As for apparel": Richard Foster, *Celebration of Discipline* (San Francisco: Harper & Row, 1988), p. 90.

page 139   "showplace of God's greatness": Dallas Willard, *Renovation of the Heart* (Colorado Springs: NavPress, 2002), p. 159.

page 140   "A cup of tea": C. S. Lewis, *The Screwtape Letters* (New York: Macmillan, 1970), pp. 86-87.

page 142   "with malice toward none": Ronald C. White Jr., *A. Lincoln: A Biography* (New York: Random House, 2009), p. 666

page 142   "sacred effort": Ibid., p. 667.

page 144   "It's an addiction": Steve Lopez, "Unwiring and Reconnecting," *Los Angeles Times*, April 29, 2009, p. A2.

page 144   the teacher found: Steve Lopez, "The Rigors of Life Unplugged," *Los Angeles Times*, May 6, 2009, p. A2.

page 145   "You'll say things": John Freeman as quoted by Scott Timberg, "Don't Press Send—Don't Even Log In," *Los Angeles Times* (November 8, 2009), p. E10.

page 145   "Psychologically, there's something": Ibid.

page 147   "almost without exception": Peter Walsh, *Enough Already! Clearing Mental Clutter to Become the Best You* (New York: Free Press, 2009), p. 4.

Chapter 10: Worry No Longer Necessary

page 154   "So cut out": Clarence Jordan, *The Cotton Patch Gospel* (Macon, Ga.: Smyth & Helwys, 1970), <rockhay.tripod.com/cotton patch/matthew.htm#06-28>.

page 156   "When [Jesus] urged them": Tom Wright, *Matthew for Everyone, Part 1* (Louisville, Ky.: Westminster John Knox, 2004), p. 66.

page 157   "There once was a time": Richard Foster, *The Freedom of Simplicity* (San Francisco: Harper & Row, 1981), p. 46.

page 159   When William Penn asked: *Quaker Spirituality: Selected Writings*, ed. Douglas Steere, The Classics of Western Spirituality (Mahwah, N.J.: Paulist, 1984), p. 282.

page 160   In Dorothy Day's houses: Dorothy Day, *Loaves and Fishes* (Maryknoll, N.Y.: Orbis, 1997), pp. 193-94.

page 160   She was profoundly attentive: Jim Forest, "Reflections on Dorothy Day and the Catholic Worker Movement," *Houston Catholic Worker* 28, no. 4 (2008) <www.cjd.org/paper/forest.html>.

page 161   "Above all, trust": Pierre Teilhard de Chardin, "Patient Trust," *Hearts on Fire: Praying with Jesuits*, ed. Michael Harter (St. Louis: Institute of Jesuit Sources, 1993), p. 58.

formatio
TRADITION. EXPERIENCE.
TRANSFORMATION.

Formatio books from InterVarsity Press follow the rich tradition of the church in the journey of spiritual formation. These books are not merely about being informed, but about being transformed by Christ and conformed to his image. Formatio stands in InterVarsity Press's evangelical publishing tradition by integrating God's Word with spiritual practice and by prompting readers to move from inward change to outward witness. InterVarsity Press uses the chambered nautilus for Formatio, a symbol of spiritual formation because of its continual spiral journey outward as it moves from its center. We believe that each of us is made with a deep desire to be in God's presence. Formatio books help us to fulfill our deepest desires and to become our true selves in light of God's grace.